Scheherazade's Legacy

Arab and Arab American Women on Writing

Edited by Susan Muaddi Darraj
Foreword by Barbara Nimri Aziz

PRAEGER

Westport, Connecticut
London

Library of Congress Cataloging-in-Publication Data

Scheherazade's legacy : Arab and Arab American women on writing / edited by Susan
  Muaddi Darraj ; foreword by Barbara Nimri Aziz.
    p. cm.
  Includes bibliographical references and index.
  ISBN 0–275–98176–2 (alk. paper)
    1. American literature—Arab American authors—History and criticism—Theory, etc.
  2. American literature—Women authors—History and criticism—Theory, etc.
  3. Women—Arab countries—Intellectual life. 4. Arab American women—Intellectual
  life. 5. Women and literature—Arab countries. 6. American literature—Arab
  influences. 7. Women and literature—United States. 8. Women authors, American—
  Biography. 9. Arab American women—Biography. 10. Women authors, Arab—
  Biography. 11. Authorship. I. Darraj, Susan Muaddi.
  PS153.A73S34 2004
  810.9'9287'089927—dc22   2004049571

British Library Cataloguing in Publication Data is available.

Library of Congress Catalog Card Number: 2004049571
ISBN: 0–275–98176–2

First published in 2004

Praeger Publishers, 88 Post Road West, Westport, CT 06881
An imprint of Greenwood Publishing Group, Inc.
www. praeger.com

Printed in the United States of America

The paper used in this book complies with the
Permanent Paper Standard issued by the National
Information Standards Organization (Z39.48–1984)

10 9 8 7 6 5 4 3 2 1

For Bassam and Alice Muaddi,
Aboud, Jawad, and Samy Muaddi,
and
Elias Darraj

Contents

Contents   ix

Foreword

Barbara Nimri Aziz

Inevitably, a time arrives in a people's history when a shared awakening occurs. In varying degrees of awareness, driven by the feeling that "It is up to me to tell my people's story," we begin. Or, we are compelled simply to tell *my* own story.

James Baldwin, when he emerged as a political voice, concluded that he could not accept what he once believed—that he was an interloper, that he could have "no other heritage [than White heritage] which I could possibly hope to use," and he would simply have to accept his special attitude, his special place in the world scheme. At one time, he had believed that otherwise, "I would have no place in *any* scheme."[†] Ultimately Baldwin rejected that fate and he went on to write some of the finest prose in American literature. Today, just fifty years later he has earned a place as one of America's foremost writers.

There are many similarities between Arab and African American experiences in the United States, and Arabs in general would gain much in our struggle for empowerment and recognition by studying our positions vis-à-vis the mainstream white society more closely. This applies to artists as well as community leaders.

Drawing from his analysis of his heritage and how he might negotiate the world of the African American and the dominant white culture he found so oppressive, Baldwin said, "One writes out of one thing only— one's own experience."[†] It is not easy when one finds oneself embedded in a hostile environment that is also one's beloved home. "Everything depends on how relentlessly one forces from this experience the last drop, sweet or bitter, it can possibly give. This is the only real concern of the artist, to recreate out of the disorder of life that order which is art."[†]

Facing the sweet and bitter, tussling with disorder, hate, fear, is asserting our responsibility, a responsibility we once had left to others. "Write or be written" is one of the three guiding principles set out in the mission statement of the Italian American Writers Association a decade ago. "Write or be written." It's that simple. African Americans learned this. Italian Americans as well. Now, as demonstrated in the surge of new books by our emerging writers, our Arab community has reached this conclusion.

"Write or be written." Because the histories we learn in school, the tales we hear in the street, the claims made on our behalf, all somehow miss the point. Or simply get it wrong. We are really not how others write us. At best we are invisible. What we witnessed and were taught was not and is not our heritage.

We may wait a generation to discover what we decide is an unbiased historian, or at least a talented sympathizer—Robert Fisk, Michael Moore, June Jordan, Noam Chomsky, or any of the numerous informed and courageous experts who try to set the record straight. Our story will finally find its way into the public arena, we believe. So we champion these men and women, and circulate their stories.

Ultimately however, we find that those accounts, when they appear, are never really satisfactory. They may inform, but only in a qualified way. Something is missing. Even if we do not say so, we feel it. What's missing is "me." Because those friendly appeals can never embody the intimacies—bitter or sweet—of what only we know is our life and that of our ancestors. They are never quite convincing, not to us anyway. Ultimately, perhaps, as mere secondhand attempts to reveal a people's soul, others' well-meaning attempts achieve little purpose toward the goal of giving voice to the voiceless.

Writing one's own story is not easy, as we are learning. When we take on the responsibility of recording our story, we have first to master the language. Yet, craft is not the foremost issue. Honesty and intimacy, often accompanied by some pain, face us when we really examine our truths. Frequently, writers speak about this. The best overcome it.

Then there is the wall to pull down. Given the heap of misrepresentations and the patronizing tales of Arabs penned by generations of Orientalists, politicians, and reporters, we face a barrier of half truths that we ourselves have imbibed and perhaps believed. So we have a great deal of sorting out to do. We must decide what is really true and what is false, then negotiate those and add to this our own hidden experience.

Arab descendants in America are, to a degree, colonized. Encouraged to forget our beautiful difference, we imbibe so many of the biases and distortions around us. We become ambiguous about our heritage. And a person who is equivocal or confused can never become an artist. As Baldwin points out, the process of making order from chaos is art.

When we reject the falsehoods, a void often opens before us. If I am not that alien, if not that exotic, if not that mean and incompetent, that nostalgic or warring woman others write me, what am I? Who was my *sitti*, my grandmother? What about her made her larger and more real than an American granny? I need to find out and then imprint her Arabness on everyone.

At one point in poet Naomi Shihab Nye's award-winning story, "Sitti's Secret," the little girl combs her grandmother's freshly washed hair, an uneventful gesture in a series of exchanges between the child and the old woman. It was not so for me. I recognized my Arab grandmother there. Only an Arab child could know this. How? Because my grandmother too invited me to comb her hair after she had washed it. That created a deeply intimate bond between my Sitti and me. I never heard of anyone else doing this. So when I read that passage in Nye's story, I was deeply moved, in part because I felt my heritage was retrieved. Nye's account gave me pride; it did not take anything from my own grandmother and our secret. Rather, it offered a means for me to share that special moment with all little girls in the world. Perhaps other children comb their grandmothers' hair. Because an Arab woman, Naomi Shihab Nye was the first to articulate it for me, it has greater poignancy. Art, not nostalgia, made the leap.

Today's Arab writers have the job and the will to seek out these overlooked minor details of our heritage and, with them, help us rebuild a fragmented, uncertain identity.

I believe it was Toni Morrison who once described writing as a process by which a person goes to a place and moves the dirt in order to understand why he or she is there at all. All writers are miners, sifting through the little things overlooked or abandoned or discolored by others. This is where Arab American writers are today, first going to the place and moving the dirt.

"They stole the little things from us," said the composer and singer Marcel Khalifé about the losses in his native Lebanon in the wake of Israel's invasion.[††] Historians, human rights experts, and politicians may quantify the gross violations of a ravaged people—millions and millions driven from their homelands, denied succor, leaving loved ones in terrifying circumstances. What makes one story, although no less tragic, more poignant than another, lies perhaps in the "little things" we are able to identify and recover. What we build from them may not overturn centuries of injustice, and it will not propel us into a position of dominance. But we can at least write our story. As for addressing what others write, perhaps as Baldwin concluded, "Truce . . . is the best we can hope for."[†]

Many committed Arab American personalities and experts have dedicated themselves to challenging erroneous and dangerous stereotypes of Arabs. These arguments may be useful in a court of law. They do not, however, make novels. Writers cannot dispute. But we can locate ourselves at that archaeological site, and build new stories from the little things we reclaim.

This is an exhilarating, backbreaking, long process that distinguishes a writer from others. In the new generation, it produced the memoir *Children of Roomje* by Elmaz Abinader, Diana Abu-Jaber's first novel *Arabian Jazz*, and the collection *Food for Our Grandmothers* edited by Joanna Kadi. These ventures, all three from women in our Arab American community, were early individual rivulets for what would become a virtual deluge of new poetry, plays, novels, and memoirs, all appearing in the past decade.

Why Arab women seem to be in the forefront of this rush of writing ourselves, I am uncertain. Possibly, we feel driven by the same spirit that led so many black women and Asian women and Italian women to search their lives, to dig through the hoary gravesites, to imbue little things with real importance.

Among African Americans, while the work of James Baldwin and Richard Wright are now classics of American literature, today four African American women—Toni Morrison, Rita Dove, Maya Angelou, and Alice Walker—are writers of tremendous talent and accomplishment. Through her writing, each one has expanded the boundaries of human experience. Doubtless, each in turn urges other women to search, to confront, and then to write. From our Asian and Indian writers, Maxine Hong Kingston, Amy Tan, Jampa Lahiri and Bharati Mukerjee have likewise have made a whole people visible and passionate.

Every generation of writers who make a social and literary impact do so by leaping barriers. Perhaps in the case of African Americans of the mid-twentieth century, it was the confrontation on race that propelled the debate into literature. While race is still a major theme in so much contemporary writing by African American writers, Morrison's work reaches into spheres of human exchange that take the African American experience and every reader to new heights, accompanied by a completely distinctive music in her language.

Can the writing of Arabs in America do this? And will we build on foundations laid in English by Khalil Gibran, Sam Hazo, or Gregory Orfalea, or in Arabic by Adonis, Nizar Qabbani, and Mahmoud Darwish?

Or will we construct our truths on the wings of Americans like June Jordan and Sonia Sanchez?

In her poem, "first writing since," the incomparably forthright poet Suheir Hammad records her news about the World Trade Center disaster of September 11, 2001, with the words "please god, let it be a mistake . . .

please don't let it be anyone who looks like my brother. . . ."[†††] There is surely not a single Arab or Muslim man or woman anywhere who, sharing that awesome news, did not utter the same thought. Yet, we needed this especially honest woman, this young writer, Suheir Hammad, to articulate that simple fear. Her words reach all men and women, universally, who at one moment in time or another, have cried "Please god, not my brother."

Hammad's work represents an important step away from nostalgia and toward a face-to-face maturity of what it is to be Arab and American. The protest novels of black writers was critical to the emergence of the African American literary voice of the twentieth century. The anger of feminists linking the personal with the universal was also a stage in their emerging voice. And Indian American writers like Jhumpa Lahiri articulate the delicate, tragic edge of their people's existence in American society.

Thus far, for the most part, Arab American writers, although we feel tormented and confused, whether by our ancestry or our tenuous place in American society or the injustices in Palestine, expose little of the real conflicts we face. Our writers seem to be struggling to tolerate, to cleanse our image, to move on. I doubt if we can really advance without openly confronting the ills that afflict us, the barriers that confront us, internal and external. We are the opposite of the angry young artist at this point in our journey.

Yet, we are on course. More young Arabs are studying literature seriously with the view to mastering the skill of writing. This, together with a greater readiness to examine ourselves and enter the heap of history that lies all around us and to move the dirt and paw through fragments reclaims the little things, and invents the rest.

Notes

[†] James Baldwin, Autobiographical Notes, in *Notes of A Native Son* (Boston: Beacon Books, 1955), 7.

[††] Marcel Khalifé, from his talk at the National Convention of the Arab American Anti-Discrimination Committee, June 9, 2000.

[†††] Suheir Hammad, "first writing since," published in *Sojourner*, November 2001.

Acknowledgments

I owe thanks to several people for the final product you hold in your hands. First, and foremost, are the twelve writers represented here. Their work is extraordinary, and I am honored to have been able to work with them to bring this collection together.

I also am grateful to Barbara Nimri Aziz, who contributed the Foreword. Barbara's many efforts, including the work she does with RAWI, to further the Arab American literary community are extraordinary. She also gave me terrific advice on this project and has been a mentor in many ways. Many thanks also to Kim Jensen, who carefully read through the draft of this book and offered her invaluable editorial advice. I also want to thank Suzanne Staszak-Silva, at Praeger Publishers, for all her help and guidance in bringing this project to fruition.

My thanks go especially to my husband, Elias Darraj, for his support throughout the process of completing this project, for helping me to find a room in which to write, and for inspiring me always.

Introduction

Susan Muaddi Darraj

In her essay, "Toward a Black Femisist Criticism," Barbara Smith wrote, "How much easier both my waking and my sleeping hours would be if there were one book in existence that would tell me something specific about my life. . . . Just one work to reflect the reality that I and the Black women whom I love are trying to create."[1]

As an Arab American woman, born and raised in the United States with a hybrid cultural consciousness, I know how Smith must have felt as she put those words on paper. I, too, often wished for a book that could speak to my experiences as both an insider and an outsider my entire life; while Americans thought I was a "foreigner," Arabs regarded me as "Americanized." I wished I could invite friends to my parents' house without getting slightly alarmed looks from them when the stuffed grape leaves, *magloubeh* (spinach and rice), or *foul* (crushed fava beans) appeared on the dinner table. How could I tell anyone that I owned cassette tapes of both Fairouz and Madonna and sang to the lyrics of both with equal zest? Most of all, who would be able to understand that I was pretty sure I was a feminist, though not completely certain because Betty Friedan and Gloria Steinem seemed to be speaking to my white classmates, not to me?

Yes, like Smith, I also needed to find that book, and the sooner the better.

I doubted its existence, however, simply because I knew that the voice of the Arab woman had been warped since it first made its way westward. Scheherazade, the heroine of *The Thousand and One Nights*, had suffered terribly at the hands of translators. Revered in the East as a heroine for distracting the sultan Shahrayar from his murderous rampage with intriguing stories (giving us "Aladdin and the Magic Lamp" and "Sinbad the Sailor"), Scheherazade became nothing more than a harem sex kitten when Antoine Galland, and later Richard Burton, introduced the *Nights* to the European canon in the eighteenth and nineteenth centuries. An intelligent woman, schooled in literature, philosophy, and history, reduced to an erotic, shallow, sex-crazed body behind a veil—it happened many times, with many Arab and/or Eastern women, including Cleopatra, Khadijah, and Aisha.

What I needed was the voice of an Arab woman to speak the truth without the filter of translation, without the influence of others sliding in to corrupt her story, because her story was possibly mine as well. Her story might describe my own confusion about feminism, marriage, education, ambition, identity, and obstacles.

I needed that story as badly as Smith needed hers, but I doubted that anyone had yet written it.

Then, one day, during the summer of 1998, I found it on the shelf at the local bookstore. I was actually reaching for a novel by another writer when my eye fell upon the Arab-sounding name on the spine, so I pulled it out. The cover, featuring a lovely, dark-haired woman wearing thick gold bangles, caught my attention, as did the quote from the late Edward Said (every young Arab American's hero) on the cover, praising the novel and the author. It was *In the Eye of the Sun*, by Ahdaf Soueif, and I sat down at the café in the bookshop to skim the first chapter. Minutes later, I purchased the book, hopped into my aging Toyota, and sped home to curl up on my sofa with this eight-hundred-page treasure. A few nights later, I closed it, smiling in relief because I had finally stumbled across the book that spoke my story, perhaps not in its details, but in its spirit.

I mentioned Soueif's novel to many friends and acquaintances who were also Arabs; not surprisingly, many of them had read it and experienced the same feeling. Someone had peered into the cavern of our innermost thoughts, and poured our story out on paper. Women especially related to it, perhaps because of the honesty with which Soueif describes sexual politics in the Arab family and society: the pressure to marry, the emphasis on having children, issues of control within marriage, the development of a feminist consciousness. Soueif's was an insider's view—the view of someone who understood, who "got it."

The discovery of Soueif led me down the path of other literature by Arab and Arab American women, including Ghada Samman, Hanan Al-Shaykh, and Naomi Shihab Nye. They became my circle of support as I struggled to crystallize and articulate my own voice. When I moved into my new home, they moved with me, settling into the shelves of my new office. When I felt disconnected from either half of my identity, their words helped me find my way. When I questioned my feminism and my own strength, they reminded me that Arab women are always strong, always resilient. When I despaired at ever fitting in, ever finding my true voice, they reminded me that my identity is to be found somewhere in between the two worlds I call home.

I am not the only one to benefit from their work. These writers have inspired many Arab women (and men), who feel trapped and caught between worlds, where the Middle East is a not-too-distant home, but America or Europe is still not a completely comfortable one. Their work helps us to find a home within that middle space, to define their own voice, and to never stop moving forward. The title of this book, *Scheherazade's Legacy*, is a testament to the heroine of *The Thousand and One Nights*, who saved the kingdom from a tyrannical monarch by weaving together her dazzling stories; in doing so, she also helped save the sultan himself, helping him see the evil of his actions and restoring his faith in humanity. The stories of Scheherazade are known around the world. Likewise, while these writers in this collection are inspired by their Eastern connections, their writing and their themes touch a global audience while reclaiming the image of Scheherazade as a woman who wove a marvelous tapestry of tales.

Here they are: each one wrote her thoughts about writing, complemented by a sample of her work. I have organized the chapters thematically. While all the essays are about writing, they naturally encompass other general themes as well: the most prominent of these were identity, politics, inspiration, memory, and language, all of which affect the writer, the writing process, and outcomes of writing in a variety of ways.

As you will notice, many of the essays also share more specific themes in common. Many find Scheherazade to be a common ancestor, the storyteller who saved a nation and healed its king. The relationships between the writers and their mothers and grandmothers—and for some, with their fathers—is another prominent theme, one that explores how they trace their affiliation with their Arab culture, how Arabic words, gestures, family traditions, and sayings create and reinforce their identity. From a political and social standpoint, many of these writers also find the crisis in Palestine to be a central issue to their identity, something not uncommon for many Arabs who view the occupation of the West Bank and Gaza as a form of colonization over the Arab people. Palestine shapes their consciousness, and it affects their views on social justice, on racism, on dispossession.

And yet, while some of their themes overlap, many of the stories, experiences, and styles of these writers are quite different. The steady, reflective voice of Naomi Shihab Nye, for example, stands in contrast to the hip, edgy voice of Suheir Hammad, and both are unlike the pensive, pondering style of Elmaz Abinader. The multitude of styles testify to the variety of ideas, opinions, and experiences within the community of women writers of Arab descent, a fact that tears down the stereotype of Arab women as uniformly similar: silent, acquiescent, unthinking.

Their voices have never been collected; these essays on writing—and how it embodies memory, politics, culture, identity—appear here for the first time. My hope is that this book will be enjoyed not only by students studying multicultural and women's writing, but by anyone who, curious to learn more about the themes that drive the literature of women of Arab descent, requires a bridge to reach "the other side"—and especially for those who have often found themselves stranded somewhere half-way across.

Note

1. Barbara Smith, "Toward a Black Femisist Criticism," in *The Truth That Never Hurts: Writings on Race, Gender, and Freedom* (New Brunswick, NJ: Rutgers University Press, 1998).

Identity

Poetry Is My Home Address

Mohja Kahf

Introduction

As with many other Arab American creative writers, Mohja Kahf's work spans several genres. In addition to being a poet, she is also an academic writer, a scholar of postcolonial and comparative literature. Born in 1967, in Syria, she emigrated with her family to the United States from Damascus at the age of three. The family settled in Utah, and her father earned his Ph.D. in Economics from the University of Utah while her mother completed a B.S. in Pharmacology. Mohja followed this scholarly path and herself earned a Ph.D. in Comparative Literature from Rutgers University in 1994.

Kahf is currently associate professor at the University of Arkansas in Fayetteville, where she teaches comparative literature, Arabic literature, postcolonialism, and literary theory. Her first book was an academic study of the image of Muslim and Arab women, entitled *Western Representations of the Muslim Woman: From Termagant to Odalisque* (1999). Her other scholarly work includes several articles in journals and anthologies, including studies of the memoirs of Huda Sha'rawi, a famous Egyptian feminist, and the literature of Arab and Muslim women.

Emails from Scheherazade (2003) is Kahf's first book of poetry. The motif of Scheherazade is one used often by Arab American women writers, as a rebuttal to the common usage of the famous *1,001 Nights* heroine in works by Western writers that portrayed Arab and Muslim women in passive and submissive roles. Modern writers like Kahf revitalize Scheherazade and restore to her image the strength, ingenuity, and imagination that she has always enjoyed in the Middle East. Kahf has published poems in *Mizna*, *PEN International Bulletin*, *The Paterson Review*, and the anthology *The Space between Our Footsteps* (1998), edited by Naomi Shihab Nye. She is married to the writer Najib Ghadbian, and they have three children.

~-~-~-~-~

In my twenties, I never wrote for my children, or about them. Friends would ask where my children were in my poetry. Poetry was mine, like my maiden name Kahf, which I have kept, as Arab women traditionally do. (Yes, it's my father's family name, but in my marital context, it's mine alone, setting me apart from my husband and children.)

Nowadays I am in full-blown mother-goddess mode and write a lot for my children. I don't mean children's books (although I have tried my hand at those, and produced hideous results). It is for the higher intelligence of my children I write, for the part of them that lives in a soul dimension where we speak as peers. My new manuscript, a prose fiction work, began for my daughters. It came out of a conversation with my eldest and flowed onto paper because I wanted to tell her and her sister something important. A few months into the writing, I got pregnant. My new son is now also part of what motivates me to write.

Here's the thing: I have to teach them something that is true and arm them against what is bogus. I can't give them grand master truths that I no longer believe in, other people's insistence that this is how the world is. The only thing I know to do is give them my honest voice, not because it is big, or perfect—it's small and imperfect, although hopefully a blast-and-a-half to read—but because it's what I have. Writing is the way I know how to be in the world, although there are other equally worthy ways to communicate and to create beauty and truth.

Long before I had this mother gig going on, writing was my thing. When I got picked on at school, I kept a journal. When a friend's mother died, I scribbled my shock into a spiral notebook. When someone pisses me off, I write them a letter, usually a not-to-be-mailed letter, but sometimes I've actually mailed it, and had both bad and good, and on occasion even life-changing, results come of those writing experiences. I've sent gushing fan letters to writers whose work delighted me (and sometimes they've written me back, to my surprise and pleasure). When I'm happy, or outraged, or depressed—when I'm traveling by plane—or by car, or staying home—when I've had a new adventure, or an illness, or a breakup, or not—I write. Writing is like chocolate, always appropriate. I used to think it was this way for everybody, but then I found out some people do things besides write as a way of coping with life. Words are my thing.

I was raised in America on the traditions of the Prophet Muhammad and the narratives of his Companions. Among them, Aisha was the most appealing to me when I was a girl, not so much Aisha as beloved wife but Aisha as a woman of eloquence and nerve. I was a girl who was constantly getting in trouble for what my family called my "long tongue," Arabic idiom for "lip," as in "Don't you give me no lip, girl." "That long tongue of yours needs to be cut," people used to scold. But it seemed to me that that Aisha girl had lip too. What's more, she backed it up with substance, with smarts. Aisha could read and write in an age when most men, let alone women, could not. She had medical knowledge gleaned from midwives and nurses and female kin, was versed in the lore of pagan Arabia, and became the foremost narrator of hadith in the early Islamic era. She had an eye for controversy, was drawn to thinking contrapuntally, and got into plenty of trouble of her own. My father encouraged me in this Aisha fascination not only by engaging me in intellectual debate in the car and at the dinner table, but by returning again and again to Aisha's famous stand in this argument, Aisha's bold words in that one. It was only natural, given my Aisha-model upbringing, that I joined the debate team in junior high school, did the announcements in high school, wrote for a newspaper in college. Even after I moved on from the Aisha model, I gravitated toward other figures who used words as their preferred mode of action in the world, such as the gaily irreverent, sensual twelfth-century Arab woman poets of Muslim Spain—Wallada bint al-Mustakfi and Mohja of Cordoba. (Yes! I have a namesake who was a poet. My name, given to me by my mother's mother, is not very common, so that happy coincidence delights me.)

I first learned what poetry was in Ms. Nowak's AP English class, senior year of high school, where the evening was spread out against the sky. I first learned how a poem is written in Enid Dame's creative writing class in college at Rutgers University, where Lillith (the first woman, created before Eve) lives. The first poem I memorized was Robert Frost's "The Road Not Taken" in sixth grade. Or was it "I Know an Old Lady Who Swallowed a Fly" by Anonymous when I was six, which I pranced around the living room singing for a guest? Or was it when I was four and memorized my first small suras from the Quran? But the Quran is not poetry—good Muslims are supposed to be adamant about this—but it is highly poetic anyway. I can still recite all these firsts, to where they bend in the undergrowth.

When I was fifteen and wrote a poem that won first place in a writing contest sponsored by the New Jersey Institute of Technology ("Grandfather," which is in my book E-mails from Scheherazad), my parents were delighted. "There's an Arabic saying," my father said, "the first part of it is sexist but listen to the rest anyway: 'The tribe is overjoyed at three things—the birth of a boy, the foaling of a mare, and the emergence of a poet.'"

"But I've been writing poetry since I was ten," I said.

"Yes, but now you are born to the world as a poet."

I don't know if that was my birth as a poet. Years later, I know I moved from a place where poetry was one sidebar among many in my life, to poetry as my home address. I had three helpers in this move: a muse, a friend to hold up a mirror of truth, and a community to provide both venue and fertile environment full of other writers and artists and lovers of poetry.

The Muse

I fall in love with one thing, feast on it ravenously, and it becomes my wake-up call to a new dimension of reality and the catalyst for a whole ream of poetry. The muse is not necessarily the inspiration, but what prepares you for the inspiration, rakes the dirt of your soul till it's ready to be seeded. My first muse was a major poet. I had always known his work but one morning I fell in love with it, I began to devour it, it began to work a fantastic sorcery on me, each poem of his peeling off another layer of reality for me, making me see every physical thing in my field of vision with new eyes: a thick tanned arm, with a man's silver watch on its wrist, hanging out of the driver's window of the car ahead of me; the body, half-turned, of a woman reaching for something on a high shelf, unconscious of her beauty; a white cat on a green lawn. The mystery of eros and human creativity glistened under every skin. Everything, everything was full of wine shimmering under its surface; I went around delirious, drunk, high.

This was the gift of that particular muse, a great poet of the body and of sexuality. I never met him in person, but he was the poet who taught me that poetry was where I lived, not just a street I was crossing.

I have learned that the muse comes to me, becomes my night and day for a time, then passes, but not before transforming and expanding my world permanently. Then there is a waiting for the next muse, alert, sniffing the air, putting yourself in the way of possibility. My next muse was not a person but a tree-sit. One lone tree-sitter, a graceful and spirited woman willing to be the lightning rod for a civic protest in my Arkansas hometown, captured my attention and a community-wide environmental effort sustained it. My ecological consciousness was raised and over the next few months I was drawn into a movement that helped put a new mayor in office to protect the natural beauty and balance of our small city. More importantly for my writing, that summer I was given new eyes and suddenly the magnolia-and-redbud landscape of my street, my hilly Ozark town, came alive, everything was a seed, and the miracles of greenery and growth opened before astounded me like dinner-plate dahlias. Back in New Jersey, where I started out, it was people energy that engaged my writing. I wanted to write the scenes of my New Jersey that had never entered any literature, like the multiethnic Muslim wedding scene I describe in "Lateefa," against the sometimes tense, sometimes joyous multiethnic grid of New Jersey itself, bursting with different generations and races of immigrants. I read Jersey poet William Carlos Williams's *Paterson* and wanted to write my Paterson, loved Walt Whitman's exuberant, sensuous parade of American people and wanted to add mine to the catalog, people who had never been in any photo album of America, like the woman who is the subject of "My Babysitter Wears a Face Veil" or the grandmother in "My Grandmother Washes Her Feet in the Sink of the Bathroom at Sears."

Muse moments come like unexpected gifts. They are invigorating for poetry, and, incidentally, great for the sex life—there is definitely a connection between writing and sex, or creativity and sex. Also between prayer and creativity, because deep creativity comes from the same place as prayer, and passionate sexuality is in there somewhere with them—in fact, I believe in a trinity of creativity, sexuality, and spirituality that ought to be the subject of an essay all its own. But not now, because I don't understand it fully. Alas, most of the time I am between such dramas, doing a different kind of writing work, steadier, diligent, careful. Doing a lot of editing and revising, and sending stuff out and filing away rejection letters and revising and sending out again. And doing the work of arranging readings and performances, and hoping to meet my next muse, or to have the breath knocked out of me by a poet's vision, at one of them.

Then there are harder times, phases when it feels as if poetry has abandoned me. As if I have no right to it. My voice withers in my throat. Every sentence I begin to pen seems derivative, inauthentic. Worse, I don't even feel like holding a pen. I used to get worried and depressed during those periods and even now they are not my best times. Once I stayed that way for two years. Nothing. But there is a winter when the trees are bare but it's then that they are absorbing nutrients; and there is a summer when they put on a glorious show. It's okay to lie low and not write. I find other activities—time with my children, a challenging university teaching career, married life and friendships, a house that needs painting and organizing, a yard that needs hostas and yuccas, and a lively community life, that is not hard—and busy myself in them. I read up on carpentry and cars. I learn a new way to peel a mango. I road-trip to the planetarium in St. Louis, and dig up distant cousins and ferret out their family stories. I listen to torrents of music. The muse will come again.

The Friend

I was lucky to have a friend who was a friend to the poetry in me. She had an eye for quality, could tell me (if I was willing to hear) when the object of my transports was worthy and when I was falling for a glitter that was not gold. She knew about creativity and how to nurture it. When the first muse hit me, I was overcome. I couldn't sleep, couldn't eat. All I wanted to do was gorge on poetry, the reading and the writing of it. I couldn't get my hands on enough poetry to read. I stayed up till all hours writing out responses to what I was reading. I had children who needed care, and here I was, a poetry junkie. I could hardly get my work done—my other work, the kind for which I get paid a salary (and which finances a room of my own in which to write).

"What do I do?" I asked her. "I'm in a state!" My friend knew about states. Creative states and spiritual states have common characteristics and require the help of a teacher or guide, for best effect.

"Don't waste it," she said. "Don't fight it. Ride the wave. Revel in it! These other things will take care of themselves."

She also said, "Be careful. Eat. Sleep. Take care of your children. Take care of work."

And I learned how to do both. How to ride the surge and not be washed away by it. How to work while keeping the poetry in my gut, and how to take it to an appropriate place, then let it out like primal joy. How to let it infuse everything I do, like love.

The work got done, somehow. The children got fed. And the poetry came streaming out.

The friend is whatever teaches you how to honor the poetry in you. The friend is a realist and deadly honest and a connoisseur of terrific writing, and an idealist who sides with paradox and unattainable goals and surrender to mystery. The friend understands that the creative life is not a frill. The life of the heart and the mind and the spirit, also not frills. They are real, maybe more real than the workaday world, and deserve your purest energy.

The Community

Once I became seriously invested in writing, I got serious about listening to criticism, opening my work to the scrutiny of an audience, and working on craft. All these outpourings needed a place to go and be heard. And I needed to be around other writers. Artists need to be around other artists at work. Poets need poets. For years I have been part of an Ozark Poets and Writers' Collective that holds monthly open mikes attended by a lively group of poets, writers, musicians, painters, journalists, songwriters, sculptors, actors. This is a venue where I can share my work, put it up for reaction, criticism, response. Be inspired by other writers' work and respond to it, engage in creative dialogue and conversation across artistic genres. There are also writing workshops and writing groups in which I revise, revise, revise. (I never stop revising. There is always room for tweaking, and even after a poem is published, the itch to revise doesn't subside. There is almost no poem I've published that I don't wish I could take back and improve, if just to snip a little word here and change a capitalization there.)

In addition to this primary writers' community in my Arkansas hometown, there are several other communities that have been important for my writing. I was involved in a private e-mail salon with twenty or so talented and high-spirited Muslim women of varied ethnic backgrounds and careers; in one poem I call them "the marvelous women," and they are. Several of us were poets. We had no-bullshit conversations there, conducted with intelligence and sensitivity and lip and sass. From our backgrounds we forged a common lexicon, so we could talk with each other on a highly evolved level I have rarely been able to find anywhere else, about Islam and feminism and sex and the body and race and spirituality and social justice and the fucked-up state of the world and Iraq and gorgeous men and the quest for the female face of the Divine and many other topics. Many times a conversation on that listserv would turn into a catalyst for a poem. And the poem, once posted, might inspire a response poem by another woman or a witty comment and, in turn, more energetic conversation from the group. Long tongues, all of us had.

The people energy that was the wellspring or muse of my early poetry and remains part of what motivates my writing led me into two other distinct writerly communities. One is RAWI, the Radius of Arab American Writers, and the other was the Muslim Writers' Guild, where I conversed with other U.S. and Canadian Muslim writers of varying races and ethnicities, especially South Asian. The Muslim Writers' Guild is now defunct, but I am still in touch with former members, and other venues have emerged, such as *The American Muslim* journal (online), where American Muslim writing is coming into its own.

I have a feeling, based on unpublished manuscripts I know are circulating in search of a publisher right now, that this will emerge as a category on the American writing scene within the next decade or so. I am still a member of RAWI, which has burgeoned into a fertile writing community, healthily focused not on the past of Arab heritage, but on the present of our morphing, cross-fertilized, Arab American reality. The journals *Al-Jadid*, *Banipal* (out of London), and *Mizna* provide important forums for this those of us in this writing community.

I attended poetry readings at Rutgers University (where I went to school) by Alicia Ostriker and other Jewish feminists who do amazing rereadings of the whole biblical heritage, drawing out the buried female elements, and I knew that the Islamic heritage was ripe for that kind of work. Ostriker said something once about awakening to feminism, she said that it was like feeling that people were telling lies about you to the newspapers. She said that she wrote poetry to tell the truth of her existence as a woman that was not being told anywhere. I remember thinking, that "everyone-telling-lies-about-you" bit, that's what being a Muslim woman is like too. That kind of personal truth telling about an unrecognized or misrecognized part of reality motivates my poetry too. In grad school I found a supportive context for that by participating in a women of color reading and other student poetry readings. I attended poetry readings by Rutgers professors Cheryl Clarke, a black feminist whose poetry was so lesbian sensual it made my eyes pop, and Abena Busia, who performed in traditional Ghanaian dress just as I often perform poetry in garb that is visually distinct, and who was a great example of how to carry that off, how to dramatically and unabashedly be that immigrant-princess-diva-poet I so love to be at times.

Once a journalist who was supposed to be reviewing my poetry reading reviewed my mode of dress instead. All she could find to say was "Here's this woman in hijab who reads poetry! Look, she's in hijab and reads poetry!" She led with it and mentioned my physical appearance about five times in her article. I found it very condescending, as if women who wear hijab were porcelain dolls who couldn't possibly be expected to know how to wield words: My, my, isn't it amazing that this one does. Millions of women around the globe wear hijab and go about their daily lives, as they do in saris and dashikis and other non-Western dress, so it's silly and ethnocentric to trip over it like that. I also found the journalist's preoccupation with my garb to be dismissive of my poetry; and ultimately, it's about the poetry. I like hijab; it connects me sensuously and sartorially to worlds of women (including my mother and my mother's mother) with whom I would not give up that mark of connection, but it is not the be-all of my existence (nor do I share the belief of many of those women in it as an essential component of being Muslim). I have read poetry in hijab and I have read without hijab, and I am happy to say the poetry goes over with audiences regardless of how I appear.

The poets I heard at Rutgers, and many others since then, have shown me by their examples how to walk this interesting landscape, of being a poet and a feminist from a minority community defensive about its sexism because it faces stereotyping and violent attack from the mainstream. How to be a woman warrior and not let either side shut you up. On one side, the people who say you should just be a poet already and write sestinas about the sunset and not write about your roots or your Muslim headcover, how gauche, stop disturbing our comfort zone. And on the other side, the people from your roots community who want you to shut up about the sexism and the bullshit within that community, and be an ambassador of the pretty side of the heritage culture. They're afraid that the FBI and the INS will use your poem, exploring the mental structure of rationalization that some Arab teenagers deploy in justifying suicide bombings, to deport your uncle, or that the Baptists will use your art that is critical of Islam and Muslims to convert your cousins. Those are the Muslim and Arab communities' versions of the debate in African American communities over Alice Walker's portrayal of domestic violence and abusive black men in *The Color Purple*. What makes it hard is that the bigotry and attack is, of course, real, and in the Muslim and Arab cases, currently getting worse— the threat of deportation is there, the community is not making it up: look at the tenured Muslim university professor in Florida who got fired for his politics; look at the suspension of rights of visa holders and residents and even naturalized citizens like me, under the frighteningly broad new anti-terrorism laws. It's not make-believe. But if you let the wrongdoing of others muzzle you, or make a defensive, lying, sugarcoating artist out of you, someone who only says what the community wants you to say, then the hatemongers win, because they will have retarded the development of art in your community.

So there can be a hazardous undertow to community too. The ultimate Muslim community weapon in this urging the artist to self-silencing is the Salman Rushdie affair: you don't want to be a cultural traitor like him, do you? It hangs—very tacitly, very subtly, usually—over the head of all Muslim artists. But you know what? The dark side of who we are will not stay covered up, nor does it help us to cover it up, and asking the disturbing, subversive questions is a noble jihad. Fear is not a basis for any art and never can be.

In spite of all that, it is still okay to write a poem about your cat. Sometimes social justice and feminism and community politics need to chill and let a gal take her woman-warrior helmet off and find poetic bliss in a bowl of fruit. Pure self-indulgent aesthetics is good clean fun. Minority artists are just as entitled to it as anyone else.

I follow Julia Cameron's prescriptions for writing in *The Artist's Way* religiously, which is to say, I am a lapsed Cameronite. But her program of three handwritten morning pages every day and a new experience or "artist's date" every few weeks serves me excellently when I follow it. It's just that at times like now, for example, when I am too groggy in the morning from 2:00 A.M. and 4:00 A.M. feedings of a wailing newborn to think straight, much less write three pages, I have to squeeze in writing time when I can (and keep notebooks everywhere for that purpose, in the car, in the kitchen, they keep getting lost under things but eventually I find them again and turn the scratch-poems into drafts). I have a friend who wrote poems about labor between contractions—now there is a marvelous woman! I am writing parts of this with one hand while my other hand supports the baby's head as he sleeps in a sling across my lap. Women have always written at the kitchen table, written wherever they could, between interruptions, and wielded the word in societies, from Sappho's to Aisha's to ours, amidst powerful other claims on their creative energies. Poetry needs friends and nurturing and a room, but it is also a potent force that will out.

A familiar comes to me in dreams; she is a tiger, an enormous, magnificent white tiger. In the dream she pads through my house. My adrenalin pumps; here is this great beast, I can see the ripple of her sinews as she skulks around my kitchen table, where my little children sit, incredibly vulnerable, and my heart is in my throat, but she doesn't touch them. She slinks between an upholstered chair and a table lamp, her thick tail brushing glass stemware, miraculously leaving it intact. She slopes through an ordinary narrow door frame, her fearful form dwarfing the scale of my house, and the musculature of her neck is liquid, the flesh of her forelegs heavy. I follow her, my heart thumping with every thud of her powerful haunches; where will she go next? What will she choose to do? She could rip the whole place apart if she wanted to. But she doesn't. She leaps with long, sinuous grace through an open window, and I now can see her lurking in the backyard, pacing dangerously on the tame green lawn and sending out signals to her kind everywhere. Suddenly she is wearing dark sunglasses, which shows she has a sense of humor. She prowls, and sniffs the air, and opens her ferocious jaws, just testing her strength. I wake up in sweat and I know this is Poetry, and she lives at my home address.

Poems

Nursing the Miracle

All I know is since I found you,
everything I touch turns to poetry

And the springs of poetry
had been dry for so long
and I was in the desert of my days
doing one of those scenes,
you know them well,
back of hand to tragic forehead,
"Will I ever write again?"

And I was down
in the dark cave, down so deep
light seemed a scientific impossibility.

I thought the numbness was death taking over
Turns out it was the stillness
you need to hatch a new self
Turns out it was all preparation

And now the water in the pool
turns to poetry. The diving board,
as my feet leave it, springs into poetry
My husband's chest hair curls
into black and white poetry
The school lunches I pack for my children
turn to poetry in their paper sacks,
and for peanut butter to turn into poetry
is very unusual

I have had this experience before
once, god, a million years ago,
and I know what a miracle is when I see it,
and I know how to nurse it,
how to guard it with both hands
the way a drunkard guards a drink
I recognize the voice of my muse
when I hear it, and know the scent
of my animus in the dark bed

Standing Amazed at the Foot of Every Tree

I stand amazed at the foot of every tree
The down on the throat of a wolf cub staggers me
I am knocked off my feet by the red belly of a robin

Every mote in the air has a story, every cell
in a leaf has a system for converting light to energy.
I stand amazed at the foot of every tree

My amazement is a new weight; I'm like a mime
tottering under invisible stacks of boxes
I am swept off my feet by the red belly of a robin

I can't walk even a block from my home
any more with a pretence of normalcy:
I halt, amazed, at the foot of every tree

Ever see a kid on his first trip to the boardwalk,
how he pitches from roller coaster to taffy counter,
then notices the fireworks, knocked off his feet?

When I think I'm done marveling, the bristling life
that's been there the whole time, only then hits me
and I stand amazed at the foot of every tree

I pitch from thicket into stream. How had I
never noticed leaf cells turning light to energy?
I am brought to my knees by the red belly of a robin,
I stand amazed at the foot of every tree.

A Woman Who Reads Poetry

I'm in bed with you
—that is, with your books,
with your writing,
your poetry—

Maybe I'm in my slip
—maybe not—
I am enjoying this
Are you?
This is how reading
should be

Day is drizzling
down my windows
The cloud of the world
is taking the fantasmic shape
of each of your poems
in turn

All good poets
re-create the world
Homer makes my husband's thighs
one an Iliad, one an Odyssey,
gives me a war
to have between them
and a well-manned ship to ride

I'm quite respectable,
normally
and very, very
literary
I don't bring every book I read
home with me
No, not every volume
I hold between my hands
makes me thrash my legs and scream

I'm no slattern
but my self slips off
as I sink deeper
into your poetry
Reading-induced visions
take hold of me
and I sob and lose my grip
on all the things that bind me
to my name as I have known it,

to my life as I have lived it,
to work, faith, family
Reading like this is sinful,
or it ought to be

I'm no drunkard
but my old knowledge staggers
under the influence
of your wine of words
I lap up cup after cup
and tear my contracts and papers
and hold my head and moan

My children trail in and out,
breakfastless
When will I admit
addiction, helplessness,
"mommy is a poem junkie"

When will I stop convulsing,
reaching for another page,
more, turning, more

of the sharp beautiful stuff
I need in my veins—damn you!
You ought to be outlawed—
but don't you ever stop
bringing it to me—

When will I sober up
from this hit
of your poetry?

~·~·~·~·~

Read me, my lady
Read me well
for I am in search
of a moonstruck reader
who will slip my poetry
on her wrists like bracelets
and see the world
take the shape of a poet
Be drunk on me, my lady
            —Nizar Kabbani*

*Excerpt from "Grant Me Love That I May Bloom and Green," by Nizar Kabbani. Translated from the Arabic by Mohja Kahf. Published in *Grand Street*, 68 (1999): 106–111.

E-mail to the Muse

Lisa Suhair Majaj

Introduction

Lisa Suhair Majaj is a writer and a scholar of Arab and Arab American literature. Born in Hawarden, Iowa, in 1960, she is the daughter of a Palestinian father and an American mother. She earned her B.A. in English from the American University of Beirut, and two M.A.s (in English and American Culture) from the University of Michigan; she is currently completing a Ph.D. in American Culture at the University of Michigan.

Her work is not limited to any single genre: critical writing, poetry, and creative nonfiction. She has coedited three books of literary criticism: *Going Global: The Transnational Reception of Third World Women Writers* (2000, with Amal Amireh); *Intersections: Gender, Nation, and Community in Arab Women's Novels* (2002, with Paula Sunderman and Therese Saliba); and *Etel Adnan: Critical Essays on the Arab American Writer and Artist* (2002, with Amal Amireh). The latter, a study of Adnan, an important Arab-American writer whose work is also represented in this anthology, is one of the first in-depth critical studies of a contemporary Arab American writer.

Majaj has published poetry and creative nonfiction in various journals and anthologies, including *Mizna, Al Jadid, The Poetry of Arab Women* (edited by Nathalie Handal), *The Space Between Our Footsteps* (edited by Naomi Shihab Nye), and *Post-Gibran: Anthology of New Arab-American Writing* (edited by Khaled Mattawa and Munir Akash). She recently published a poetry chapbook, *These Words*. Her poems have been translated into Arabic and Hebrew.

Majaj currently lives in Cyprus with her husband and two children.

From: LSM (poet/writer/activist/mother/chief-cook-and-bottle-washer/
Palestinian American/human being)
To: The Muse
Subject: The Writing Life

Dear Ms. Muse,

Remember me, your friendly neighborhood (globally speaking) writer? No, don't try to pretend you can't place me. There was a time when we knew each other pretty well, you and I; it's been a while, but not *that* long. Just because I had a couple of kids, haven't slept in a few years, can't find my desk under the stacks of plastic toys and picture books and felt-tip drawings of mermaids, do you think you can move out, leave town, find another writer to visit? Well, think again. You, the queen of creativity, don't pretend you don't see the link between birthing a child and birthing a poem! Have you forgotten how you paid me a surprise visit in the middle of my labor with my second child? How you inspired me to write haiku between contractions, flooding the spaces between pain with the astonishing gift of words? Even after the baby had surged his way out of my body, leaving me as exhausted and grateful as a boat person who's crawled ashore and hasn't yet been turned over to immigration, you didn't disappear. The next morning, there you were, whispering in my ear about memory and parenthood and history and community and culture, forcing me to rummage around in my bedside table for pen and paper so that I could scribble notes over the top of my nursing newborn's head. It would have been easier to nap, but I didn't mind: I counted on you to help me make meaning out of that confusing welter of pain and joy that is childbirth. And you rose to the task, reminding me that giving birth is, in some oblique way, like going through a war: in both cases one reenters the world from a space of extremity, suffused with gratitude for what one has in one's hands, and changed utterly.

So what has happened to you lately, now that the state of the world grows grimmer by the day, stretching my soul to the breaking point, and I need poetry's lifeblood infusions more than ever? And where are you at those other moments when joy rises in me like a river, and the need for articulation rises with it? It's true, of course, that this lapse in our relationship isn't only your fault. I haven't had much time for you lately: children bring their own poetry into the world, but it's not always the kind that gets written down in words. And I suppose it must be hard work to inspire a writer who hasn't slept a full night in six years, who can't pick up a pen or turn on a computer without having someone small and utterly important demand immediate attention. But don't just turn your back and walk away, as if whatever we had going is history! Can't we at least talk?

Could it be that you're jealous? That you're comparing my current preoccupation, my lack of responsiveness to your charms, to the intensity I used to bring to our encounters? I remember the times I used to slip away from my "real" life to meet you, rationalizing our relationship in the manner of guilty lovers everywhere. You'd be seductive, alluring. I'd resist at first, but then give in to the promise of passion, letting your wild current, your torrent of sensory perceptions and images and memories carry me downstream in a mad rush, till I found myself flung at last, soaked and exhilarated, on the bank of the river—disoriented, exhausted, my lips tingling with poetry. Those were the times I'd look up with a start from the scribbled lines on the page, the humming shimmer of my computer screen, to find the breakfast dishes still in the sink as light faded in the sky, or worse, dawn seeping through the slats of my blinds after a late night stint. Sometimes I'd groan as I confronted the detritus of uncompleted tasks left behind in your wake. But the memory of our tumultuous encounter would stay with me even when I reentered the prosaic domain. And if I was lucky, I would be left with a talisman: a poem whose jagged lines I could polish smooth over time.

These days, I'll scribble half a line, then put down my pen to turn to some more pressing task, the ringing phone, the baby's cry. It's hard to plunge passionately into the river of language when you've only got time for three words. But that's where you come in: you, the Muse. Remember your job description? To motivate, to inspire! You're not supposed to fall down on the job just because there are distractions or constraints! You're the specialist, after all, in spurring people to write at odd moments, in awkward places: halfway through a shower, or in between spreading the peanut butter and the jelly. You probably have a stock portfolio heavily invested in the companies that make those tiny notebooks, the kind you can shove in a hip pocket and pull out between the canned goods and the cereal in the grocery store. Surely it's in your interest to keep the inspiration flowing!

Besides, when did you ever take convenience into consideration? You always seemed to take special pleasure in inflaming me with poetry just when the pressures of regular life were greatest and writing seemed most like an indulgence. You'd drop by as I was struggling to meet a deadline, or anxiously counting the minutes left of my child-care time, and next thing I knew some item from the news would have come together with the rain beading on trees outside my window, an odor from the neighbor's kitchen, a long-forgotten memory, and there I would be, scribbling madly in the margins of whatever I was supposed to be working on, following the crumb trail of words into thickets I had never planned to explore. It used to be downright frustrating, how you only seemed to have time for me when I was busy with other things, while the days I'd sit and wait for you, you were nowhere to be found. But don't get me wrong: I believe you when you insist that it wasn't just coyness on your part. After all, maybe the most important gift you've ever given me is this: the understanding that no matter what the situation, poetry is never truly an indulgence. Rather, it's a matter of sanity: keeping one's own, and helping to create more in the world if we possibly can.

I remember those late night visits you'd pay me. I'd be staring at my computer screen, reading endless e-mails about Palestine and Iraq and other desperate places, feeling torn into a million jagged pieces by the state of the world and by the unlikelihood that ordinary people, especially those who happened to be Arab, would ever find justice. Outside the window, snow would hush its soft way down, or the sultry dark of summer would pool on the pane. Fragments of news would batter the inner recesses of my skull like moths trapped inside a lampshade: bulldozed homes and body counts, lives ravaged by the machinations of the powerful. I'd pick up my pen or open a blank document on my screen, searching for language adequate to the facts of the day.

But a sense of helplessness would paralyze me. What use, I'd wonder, is language against the physical realities of injustice? And in the face of these realities, what right did I have to indulge myself in poems about trees or camping? Then there would be a small, subtle shift in energy— as when someone has entered a room and you sense their presence before hearing or seeing them. I'd take a breath, and on the exhale there you'd be, flooding me with words the way a hungry woman pours out rice for cooking. I'd write line after line, quickly, knowing you might disappear at any minute, every cell in my body trembling with the sheer relief of articulation. It wasn't as if you gave me poems scissored from whole-cloth, ready to be transcribed. With you, nothing ever comes that easy! But you gave me something I could work with: the raw material of language. And that was the most precious gift of all: it was what made it possible to beat back despair. Writing got me through the griefs I couldn't push aside, the images that lodged inside me and festered. If it weren't for you, I might have huddled down inside myself, stayed where it was silent and safe. Because of you, I could fight back. Because of you, I discovered my power.

I remember reading this observation by Julia Cameron (you know, the creativity expert who specializes in introducing you to people as if she were your private matchmaker): that creativity not only makes life useful to us, it makes us useful to life. That's it in a nutshell. Without you, I'm useless: brutalized by the news, helpless in the face of all that destroys our humanity on this planet. With you, life makes more sense: at least I can do something that matters, say something that might—somehow, somewhere, to somebody—make a difference. And it's a wonderful thing to be useful in this life: it makes all the jagged pieces fit together, like molecules of air flowing together in a single breath.

Because of you, too, I discovered something else: my joy. Imagine this: A woman is lost in the dark recesses of an endless cave. When she cries out her words return to her as echoes, distorted and misshapen. Then something changes: something stirs. Looking around her, she glimpses light, hears the murmur of running water. As she moves forward her excitement grows, the current of life quickening within her. Suddenly she finds herself at the opening of the cave, looking out into a vast clearing lit with sun. She calls out, her words strong and melodic. Somewhere on the other side of the clearing a voice shouts out in return. Her heart expands like light: she is not alone! She runs forward into dappled air, joy rising in her like a river. Everywhere birds are singing.

But all too often this joy, this power, are temporary. You come and then you leave: you always leave. The river sinks to a tepid trickle, dries to a cracked gully. Language shrivels to a hard dry nut. Suddenly I can't see two words ahead of me, can't write my way through a vegetable patch, much less a war zone. You get tired, I suppose, of the way the synapses in my brain fail to function after prolonged sleep deprivation; of how I'm constantly trying to squeeze you in between diapers and dishes and deadlines. You want more time and space than I can give you. No doubt there have been times you gave up on me altogether, times you were convinced that the snowy page that stared back at me would remain blank forever. I struggle to maintain an engagement with the world, to balance the hats of writer, academic, and activist while shepherding two young children through nonstop days and sleepless nights, but child rearing sucks everything into its centrifugal force field. In the face of parenthood's constant battle for those most basic of commodities—sleep, time, energy—what chance does poetry have? One can plant a nut, water it, hope it will grow. But germination takes time and patience, and something more: some life force arising from a mysterious conjunction of energies that can't simply be willed into being.

But that's where you come in—you, the expert on the mysteries of creation. You know better than anyone about that confluence of energies giving rise to new life: about the fortuitous meeting of earth and sun, artist and medium, self and world. After all, it's you who taught me to fling myself openhearted into the world and trust that a spark would be generated. And perhaps the secret of balancing writing with all the other things we do in the course of a day lies in this knowledge—that the goals of creativity, whatever the context, are remarkably similar: to enrich our lives and the lives of those around us, to imagine and create a world that is saner and more beautiful than the current one. And indeed, whether

I'm soothing a crying baby, teaching a class, applauding a first-grader's drawings, penning a poem, editing a book or marching in a protest, my actions are rooted in a conviction that, as individuals, what we say and do matters, and that birthing and nurturing, whether of children or of artistic creations, nourish us in the deepest recesses of our being—as well as helping, in some small way, to change the world.

Of course, in one way or another, you've been showing me this for years, long before I became either a mother or a writer. Perhaps you remember one afternoon when I was around eleven, when the possibilities of poetry seemed to permeate everything. My English assignment that day was to write a poem. I got off the bus and found that an unseasonal spring shower had been overtaken by sunshine. The jasmine vine twining up our front wall was beaded with rain, jeweled drops sparkling at the heart of each small blossom. The sparks of water lighting the flowers from within made me think of brilliant things: diamonds, candles, stars. Excitedly, I composed a series of small poems about the scene; each time I captured a shard of my perception in words, the world around me seemed to crystallize into something magical. Finding a verbal structure for my perceptions, for the particular beauty of that day, made me feel connected to something larger than myself: not just the natural world, but a sense of my own power. Perhaps this is the moment when I first began to understand that articulation is a form of agency, one way to claim a place in the world. The next day the garden was back to its ordinary state, the jasmine un-jeweled and a bit dusty. But I had the poems, and in some oblique way, neither I nor my relation to the world would ever be the same again.

Later that year, when my teacher, Sue Dahdah (a gifted educator whose conviction that education should nourish, not quash, the creative spirit still inspires me today) asked us to choose a project for English, I decided to write a book of poems. I still remember the adventure of wandering about with a notebook in my hand, awaiting inspiration; the excitement of filling page after page with my own poems and accompanying illustrations; the thrill of mastery as I labored to find the precise words, the exact rhythms necessary to each line. The poems themselves have (thankfully) been lost. But what has stayed with me is the sense of exhilaration that attended the act of writing: the sense that to create verbal structures was a meaningful act.

Do you remember that one poem I composed about a ravaged, stately tree, its aged branches gnarled like limbs? I no longer recall why I chose that tree as my topic: perhaps I was thinking about some ancient olive trees I'd seen in Jerusalem, whose resonance had permeated my being like the after tone of a chiming bell. At any rate, as the afternoon light faded, I wrote and wrote, scratching out lines and trying new ones, transfixed by the way one line of words branched into another, much like the branching limbs of the tree I was trying to describe. Time expanded as I wrote; it was as if the page were a doorway illuminated by light. At that moment language seemed more supple and flexible than anything else had yet been in my fairly constricted life. I had yet not heard of the Muse, but you must have been there, in one of your many guises, peering over my shoulder and smiling to yourself.

As I got older you showed me more clearly how poetry arises from the admixture of pain and beauty at the heart of any intense experience. In the manner of teenagers everywhere, I was rent by extreme emotions, and writing seemed to offer some solace. I wrote poems about love and death and God and the meaning of life, anchoring my vague philosophical flounderings with occasional details from the physical world: the smoky, pink streaks across a winter sky just before dusk, or the speckles of ash clinging to a fresh-baked egg from the *ka'ak* oven. Language was there for me when nothing else was. And when the words refused to come, as they often did, there was always reading to count on, stacks of books that transported me beyond daily life's boundaries. (Helpfully, my mother, whose love of reading inspired my own, was the school librarian, and routinely brought home new arrivals to read before shelving them. To this day I can recall the particular odor of ink and paper those new books exuded, the excitement of opening their glossy covers.)

Novels about war, especially World War II, drew me with particular intensity. Perhaps this was because I had had some experience of my own with war: the 1967 Israeli–Arab War, when Israeli bombers flew overhead and air-raid sirens rent the air; Black September of 1970, when the Jordanian army fought Palestinian militias and combat raged in our backyard; the 1973 Arab–Israeli War, when we blued out our windows and headlights in fear of air raids. I had a sense, too, of what it meant to be Palestinian, whether in Jordan or in the Occupied Territories. Unable to process the implications of these experiences, I didn't write about them until much later. But throughout my teenage years, books that pertained to war and conflict, that described such things as food shortages, blackouts, and bombings, seemed utterly relevant, and I read them voraciously.

Of course, my literary fare wasn't restricted to wartime narratives: you've always been eclectic in your influences, and for that I'm grateful. I read books about animals and nature and orphans and teen romance and girl explorers, about space travel and time travel and far-flung historical sagas. I read Dickens and Twain and Nancy Drew and Anne of Green Gables, making little distinction between "famous authors" and serial fiction. I memorized poems, both for school and for pleasure: to this day I can recite sections of "The Charge of the Light Brigade," memorized at age seven, as well as other poems whose cadences still inhabit my bones.

In college I continued my exploration of the possibilities of writing, grappling in particular with the connection between writing and war. Surely you recall our clandestine meetings during my years at the American University of Beirut, where I used to sit on rocks overlooking the sea and scribble in a tattered orange notebook, trying to make sense of the civil war that had enveloped the country. I was a teenager: vulnerable, lonely, with few resources through which to comprehend violence. You came to me in small ways, through images, colors, odors, offering language as a way to structure experience. All around me was the war: just beyond the campus boundaries, just beyond the limits of comprehension. But I couldn't write about it directly. It was too large and too terrible, and for all that I had a number of close calls during my time in Lebanon, my own experience of it was too limited. I could only write about small splinters of it, perceptions that pierced my awareness like shrapnel.

I recall, for instance, my first night in Beirut. For hours I huddled below the dormitory stairs, listening to the reverberations of artillery shells. My sister, who shared the dorm room with me, refused to come downstairs: an old hand at Beirut life, she preferred to sleep through the bombardment. When I returned at dawn to our room, she was still dozing, the pillow over her head. As the morning light stained the horizon gray, I sat by the window and wrote a poem whose constricted lines echoed the narrow space of the room behind me, the constriction in my chest. I had no clear images for what I had experienced that night, my sense of smallness in the face of terror. All I could articulate was the weight of the morning sky, the omnipresent grayness, the fact that even the staccato sound of tennis balls thudding against the tarmac of the nearby court sounded like gunfire.

Later, more direct images forced their way into my consciousness. One experience that impressed itself on me with particular clarity occurred just before I left Lebanon in 1982. The Israeli invasion of Lebanon had begun, and refugees from the battered south were flooding into the capital. I was rushing past the university hospital, trying frantically to arrange the details of my own evacuation, when through the glass windows of the emergency room I saw a man standing, swaying slightly, clutching a child to his body. The child had a wound in his forehead. Blood had dripped on the floor at the man's feet, splattering the tiles, but neither man nor boy seemed to notice: their faces were vacant masks of exhaustion. Time froze for a moment as I stood before this stilled snapshot of war. Helpless to do anything, anxious about what I had to accomplish before dark made the streets unsafe, I moved on. As I made my way down the street, I had the sensation of buildings tilting toward me, of a city on the verge of collapse. A day or two later, I left Beirut in an open truck with other refugees. Eventually, after various experiences (including the forced rerouting of our evacuation boat to Israel for interrogation), I made my way to Jordan. Physically I was unscathed. But the memory of that bleeding child, along with other memories, stayed lodged within me like a shard of twisted metal.

Shortly afterward I moved to the United States to pursue graduate studies at a midwestern university whose distance from Beirut seemed immeasurable. Gripped by terror that I would not succeed in my chosen field, I stayed up late night after night laboring over studies for which I felt inadequately prepared. There was no time for poetry, at least not for the writing of it. But during the summer term I enrolled, almost guiltily, in a creative writing course. The required journaling and free-writing exercises forced me to venture beneath the barricaded surface of my mind, and what surfaced were poems and vignettes about Beirut, the invasion, the other wars that shadowed my past. I think my classmates thought I was slightly odd: someone complained my poems were "too violent." But despite the serenade of summer outside my window, the lure of cold beer and pizza at nearby student hangouts, I could not relinquish my subject matter. Writing about the war was like breaking a skin of ice on a dark pond: there were fish below the surface, massive creatures moving silently through the frigid dark, and poetry seemed one way to reel them in, to take stock of their hulking forms and assess the threat they posed.

At the same time I discovered—or remembered—the ways in which writing offers not only a way to travel to the depths but also a way to live more fully on the surface. The more I wrote, the more poetry took me not only in and back, but also up and out. Lifting my head from the weight of winter, I found myself walking through the present, my senses alive to the world around me: a tree fleshing its bare silhouette into soft green leaf; light glinting off a wind-ruffled river; rough concrete warming the bare soles of my feet. At the time I was reading William Faulkner, Elizabeth Bishop, Robert Francis: I felt my very being saturated with the possibilities of language. I paced the sidewalks in a sort of trance, literary cadences measuring my tread. As it had on that long-ago afternoon, when rain sparked the jasmine to fire, plunging into the river of words felt like tapping into the heart of the world.

But this elation was short-lived: as seems to be your wont, you came and then you left. Working till 2:00 A.M. every night left little time for creative writing, and in any case immersion in academia soon decimated any belief I had harbored in my own literary powers. I wrote privately, in spurts, but hid my writing and didn't take it seriously. Then my mother died of cancer, and you withdrew even further away. A therapist I saw for grief management advised me to try writing in a journal, but the effort of dredging words from that ocean of pain only seemed to plunge me deeper into silence. Words could neither bring my mother back nor encompass the immensity of my loss, and so I abandoned the effort as useless. Wherever you were during that period, you hid yourself well. Perhaps this is the betrayal I blame you for most: that you saw me cast up on grief's rocky shore and left me there alone, battered and silent.

Over time, however, I slowly made my way back to writing—or perhaps it was you who made your way back to me. I wrote small poems about my mother's death, the process of articulation providing, at last, a small surcease for the pain lodged behind my breastbone. Then the first Palestinian intifada erupted, and the nightly images of bone-breaking and home-smashing made something break loose inside of me. Words began to crack the surface, like leaves sprouting from bone. When my father, too, died of cancer after a futile attempt at treatment, I found myself face to face with the Palestinian history his life had embodied. For the first time I began to see my own writing as meaningful in a broader context: to articulate some small portion of the Palestinian experience of which my father's life had been a part was, perhaps, one way of standing up in the face of injustice.

Connection sparked connection, words branching outward and then arcing back in flashes of illumination. I joined an Arab-Jewish dialogue group as well as a Palestinian online discussion group; within these forums I began to clarify my identity as a Palestinian and to experiment with a more public, more political, voice. For the first time I began sending my writing out for publication. Iraq invaded Kuwait, the United States set its deadline for war, and I joined a local activist group of Americans and Arabs working for peace. I published a poem about the intifada in a local journal, and read it—my first public poetry reading—at an antiwar event; the connection between poetry and activism that was consolidated then has energized my work ever since. Meanwhile I had begun researching Arab American literature, and had established personal contact with a number of authors. The growing sense of an Arab American literary community—a space within which I might finally feel at home—was exhilarating and empowering.

Throughout all of these developments, I now realize, you've been there, albeit often in the shadows. And what you've taught me is this: that language matters, that it makes a difference, and that we ignore it at our peril.

For all that I've railed against your absences, I'll always remember that if it weren't for you I might never have learned to stand up with a simple "no" on my lips, nor to claim my "yes"; that I might never have understood that every story begins with a single word. What you have shown me, in different ways, is this: that writing is, at its heart, a way of living in the world. It's a way to resist, to celebrate, to take action. It's a vehicle for exploration and empowerment and grief and protest and laughter. And it's one of the richest ways I've discovered of being human. For helping me to plunge into that river of language, to ride its wild and wonderful currents, I remain grateful to you. Yes, sometimes I've wished you would give me more: more inspiration, more poems, more "success." But perhaps that's not the point. After all, the writing life isn't a race to see who can stockpile the most publications. It's a matter of living with language. Poems and stories and essays are always alive within us: our job is to help give them birth, to midwife them toward the light.

Lately, I realize, you've been visiting my young daughter as well. It isn't just the poems she started dictating to me at the age of four, about flowers and mermaid stars, about her heart "walking in [her] chest because it feels happy." It's other things as well, like the scrap of paper I recently found on which she had painstakingly written, "Poery [sic] Against the War." It didn't matter that she had copied the words from a poster I had on my wall. Those crooked red felt-tip letters were the best vindication I could ever have of why poetry matters. As I hugged her, I imagined you hovering somewhere nearby, smiling to yourself at the idea that a small poet-activist might be coming to light.

These days, as the crazed agendas of demagogues make the world less and less habitable for any of us, I realize how much I depend on you to get me through. The other day, for instance, I signed onto my computer and found a report about the death of an eight-year-old girl named Aaya Fayad. Aaya, it seems, had been excitedly awaiting the start of the school year: like my own daughter, she had insisted on carrying her new schoolbag around the house, on wearing her new school clothes in anticipation of the big day. But the Saturday before, she was riding her bicycle in the Anum Sarwi neighborhood of Khan Yunis when Israeli soldiers began shooting into the neighborhood from a nearby settlement. Aaya, the report says, died instantly.

What am I to make of such news? Without you I'm helpless, bludgeoned to silence. Do I cry? Rage helplessly? I can't even call my representative to express my horror at what is being funded with my U.S. tax dollars, because I live in Cyprus and no longer have a local representative. I could walk down the street to the American embassy to protest, but if they knew my mission they would never let me through the heavy metal doors and the metal detectors and the double sets of walls and the guards and the machines that check for any trace of explosives.

It's not that I expect you to comfort me, exactly. What you do best is something else: you force me to articulate, to imagine. And from this comes action: the ability to rage purposefully. As I write, American troops occupy Iraq and Afghanistan; Israel has just passed a racist law aimed at stripping residency rights from non-Jews; the "separation wall" imprisoning Palestinians grows higher; violence routinely claims the lives of innocents; civil rights in the United States and elsewhere are sacrificed to hysteria. There's no denying that it's a dark time. And now Edward Said has died—peerless intellectual, writer, teacher, musician, standard-bearer of justice for Palestinians and upholder of the principle of justice for everyone. Without his voice, his words, his passion, his commitment, his leadership, we are all bereft.

But daily I am buoyed by my community of family and friends and fellow travelers on the planet—a global community, maintained by the grace of e-mail. Daily the faces of my children offer reasons to hope, reasons to persevere. Daily the natural world proffers its blessings. And daily I remember that there is always language to fall back on: there is always writing. I count on you, the Muse, to help me claim and honor these gifts: the ability to walk with awareness through the world, to articulate some part of what it means to be human. In the face of all that the world brings to bear, what poetry can do seems little indeed. But each time the river of language rises in me, I am able to believe, once again, that it is enough.

Poems

The Arab-American Woman Reads Poetry

The audience watches curiously
as the Arab-American woman steps up
to the podium. She is not what they expected:
light hair and skin, unaccented speech.
They thought she'd be more—you know—*exotic.*

Or else: the audience watches attentively

as the Arab-American woman steps up
to the podium. She is what they were waiting for—
cousin, compatriot, fellow-traveler,
Arab resonances in a place far from home.

But the Arab-American woman hesitates,
shuffling her sheaf of poems: meditations
coined from musk of stone, chipped particles

of light. She's weary of living on only one side
of the hyphen. Her poems aren't just translations:
this is her home, in an odd, unhomelike sort of way.
But if she blinks, someone always cries out
Look at those Arab eyes!

She wants to walk into the forest empty handed,
climb up a mountain and down again,
carrying no more than what any human needs to live.
She wants to stand alone in a high place,
send her voice echoing across wild rivers.

Already she can hear the objections:
"Do Arab women do things like that?
Don't they wear long clothes
and stay in the house, cooking?"
And the protests: "We have so many problems!
—our identity to defend, our culture under siege.
We can't waste time admiring trees!"

But the Arab-American woman has news.
She knows who she is, and its not what you think.
When she wears hiking boots and jeans
she's just as authentic
as her sister in the embroidered dress.
When she walks up a mountain, her identity goes up with her
and comes back down again.

Besides, she's learned a secret.
Two cultures can be lighter than one
if the space between them
—the space they open up—
is fluid, like a stream of light,
or wind between two open hands,
or the future, which knows how to change.

She's standing at the podium, waiting.
She wants to read a poem about walking
up a mountain. It's a poem
about memory, and culture, and heritage;
about the things you take with you,
the things you leave behind, the things you change.

It's a poem about being and becoming
about the way voices resonate from high places,
setting off echoes, reverberations

It's a poem about the future

**"What Happens Next?
Be the First to Know.
CNN Breaking News"**

Next there is asphodel, anemone,
children gathering twigs
and tadpoles. Next there are kite tails
wandering over the wide sky
of spring. Next are hen's eggs
fresh-laid and almond trees breaking
to blossom and village bread fragrant
from dome-shaped ovens of clay
and kittens mewing and seasons uncurling
like new leaves, tender and green

and next we have war.

(March 2003)

Countdown

Outside the rain keeps falling.
Glowering air, dazed
with Saharan dust, shrouds
the horizon. Wildflowers
huddle in the empty lots,
keep their heads tucked down,
their mouths snapped shut.

Yesterday we were a fingertip
from war. Today the distance is that
of a hangnail. I turn my hands over
and over, searching for some news
I can hold, but find only
calloused flesh, rough bitten skin.

Air cupped in my palms
feels heavier than grief.

My baby claps his chubby hands,
fingers splayed like stars.
He grips my forefinger fiercely
as if I were a rudder.

We are hours from war.
Only love will save us now.

My Country, My Words: Reflections of My Life as a Writer

Nathalie Handal

Introduction

It is difficult to identify Nathalie Handal only as an American poet, since she spent her formative years growing up in different parts of the world. She has lived in the United States, Europe, the Caribbean, and Latin America, and has traveled extensively in the Middle East and eastern Europe. She completed her postgraduate studies in English and drama at the University of London, and earned an M.F.A. in Creative Writing and Literature at Bennington College. She also has an M.A. in English and a B.A. in International Relations and Communications from Simmons College in Boston, Massachusetts.

Handal's writing has been published in many magazines and periodicals, and her work has appeared in various anthologies, most recently, *110 Stories: New York Writes after September 11* (2002), and *This Bridge We Call Home: Embodying the Spirit of This Bridge Called My Back*, ed. Gloria Anzaldua and AnaLouise Keating (2002). She is the title poet of an anthology edited by Naomi Shihab Nye, *The Space between Our Footsteps* (1998).

She has published one book of poetry, *The NeverField* (1999) and *The Lives of Rain* is forthcoming. She edited *The Poetry of Arab Women: A Contemporary Anthology* (2000), an Academy of American Poets best-seller and winner of the Pen Oakland/Josephine Miles Award. The collection is an important one in the genre of Arab literature, as it collects voices of Arab women living both in the Middle East and around the world.

Her plays have had readings in numerous venues throughout the United States and the United Kingdom; she has also directed several plays, most recently, *Before We Start* by Yussef El Guindi for the First Arab American Comedy Festival in

New York City. Her piece *War* has been incorporated into a theater production, *Lost Recipes*, a love song of resistance that combines the voices of multiple Arab American and Jewish American women writers.

Handal is currently working on two major theatrical productions, and is a script developer for the production company The Kazbah Project. She is also editing the anthology, *Arab-American Literature and Dominican Literature*, and coediting, along with Tina Chang and Ravi Shankar, *Risen from East: An Anthology of South Asian, East Asian, and Middle Eastern Poets*.

∽-∾-∽-∾-∽-∾-∽

It is May 2003 and I am still writing this sentence. Still trying to finish it. Still trying to interpret each word and its own particular accent. I am still sitting here, always somewhere else, but still in front of my desk, writing.

My relationship with words started when I was a tiny girl. My parents had me in 1969, they were only twenty, and part of the student revolutionaries in Europe (living mainly in Switzerland and France), before going to Boston and living the hippy era. Having come from a Palestinian background they had struggled their entire lives with place and identity; they were leftist, obsessed and rightly so, with justice and equality. They spoke endlessly about politics, world affairs, and recited passionately verses of French and Arabic literature to me. I grew up knowing every song, every word Charles Aznavour ever wrote, grew up reading Kahlil Gibran and Charles Baudelaire, especially *Les Fleurs du mal*, grew up listening to the plays of Corneille and Racine and memorizing the fables of Jean de la Fontaine. I grew up discussing with my father existential notions, issues of exile and displacement, and particularly issues of inequality and injustice. My father has always been infuriated by the injustices in the world, and he would read me passages from books and journals, showing me how man creates misery and poverty in the world, how power consumes people and how all empires eventually fall. My mother read book after book, and books were everywhere in the house. We had no country, books were our country.

I started writing creatively in high school. It was 1985, and Marie Bogart was the first teacher I had who let me explore my creative side. I let myself go with the words that came to me. I was in the Caribbean where my parents went after Boston via Miami, and there weren't any readings around town or writing workshops that could help me. So instead, I kept telling stories and I acted. I loved acting. I loved singing. I was in all the school plays. I watched movie after movie, and danced Creole folklore, ballet, jazz, and merengue.

During that time, Haiti was on the verge of an important change in its history as Duvalier was about to be ousted in 1986. The disturbances in our lives were constant—curfew after curfew, blackouts, gunshots, deaths, and not knowing when we would be able to go to school or at any given moment when we had to leave school for a safer place. Coming from a Palestinian background, political turmoil was something I grew up with. However, Haiti in retrospect, had a profound impact on me—it made me once again question how I saw myself in the world, how others saw me, what exile meant, it focused me to question humanity, issues of race, focused me to witness the horrors man commits against man, and obliged me to be aware. The images of death of that period in Haiti remain scars in my mind and I did not completely absorb them until later on.

When I got to college in Boston, I immediately became a student activist, marching/protesting during the Contra/Sandinista conflict, and helping to bring awareness to the Palestine tragedy. I did my undergraduate degree at Simmons College, which was a women's college, and started gaining awareness on women's issues. It was the first time I heard women speak out so freely about their sexuality. Observing women with the power of speech and expression empowered me tremendously. It was the beginning of my discovery of my own sexuality, of Arab feminism and accepting myself as an Arab woman who had the right to be free with her body, who could think about sex in a positive way.

During that time, I wrote, continued to read, and went to see all the plays and musicals I could. However, political issues seemed more urgent to me and becoming an actor professionally was something I never really allowed myself to dream about since I knew that my family would never accept it. But my love for writing could not leave me. I started writing poetry more and more. One day, my roommate and dear friend Danielle Balest suggested I show my English professor, David Gullette, my poems. She insisted so much, that my poems and I decided to pay him a visit.

I went into his office and told him I wanted his opinion on my poems. He looked like a character straight from a play—his silver beard, his deep voice, his dramatic gestures. I was seduced. He recited a poem for me and I knew I was where I should be. He also introduced me to literary journals and magazines—*Prairie Schooner, The Paris Review,* and so forth. Then he started critiquing my poems and since I had never been in such a situation, I took it badly. I went back to the dorm and told Danielle that I could not write. Although I was destroyed, it was temporary, and Gullette left me with something vital—an open door. A door into myself, into the world of words.

About a year after my visit to Gullette, I decided to take a creative writing class with Floyd Barbour and a Shakespeare class with Gullette. From that moment on, I never looked back. I knew that literature and writing was what I wanted to focus on. Although I ended up majoring in International Relations and Political Science, I took as many literature classes as I could. During that time, I seriously started reading Samuel

Beckett and the Irish authors, Nazim Hikmet, Anna Akhmatova, Yannis Ritsos, Cavafy, and the South American and Arab writers, especially Octavio Paz, Pablo Neruda, and Mahmoud Darwish. And I was obsessed at the time with Federico Garcia Lorca and Rumi.

I discovered Rumi at the library one day. There was this little book on the shelf calling me. I kept ignoring it but after a few hours, the battle ended and I gave in. I went to the book, took it off the shelf, and started to read. I was taken away from the very first line. During that moment in my life, my spiritual journey began. I meditated, read the Vedas, the Sufis, the Kabbalah, became interested in mythology, as well as the French surrealist writers and abstract art. What mattered most to me then was that the poem made me travel. At the time I thought that traveling was an escape, and that escape was home, but I have come to realize that traveling is home, and my house is built of words.

In Barbour's class, I wrote many plays and a crucial moment for me was when I started reading African American authors such as June Jordan, Alice Walker, and Langston Hughes. They wrote about experiences of marginalization, discrimination, and injustice, about issues I related to. But it was not until I left college that their influence really impacted my own work for I was still too consumed with trying to collect the pieces of myself.

When I finished my M.A., also at Simmons College, I left Boston and went back to Paris. There, I met many European and Arab writers and thinkers, among them Mahmoud Darwish. Through these Arab intellectuals, I learned a lot about the Arab literary scene and Arab literature in general. It was also in Paris that I discovered Arab women literature to such a large extent, and became interested in bringing these writers to the United States and also bringing Arab American literature to the attention of people in Europe and the Arab world. The Institut du Monde Arabe was an inspiring space for me because there is no other Arab cultural center of its kind. It was in Paris that I gave my first lecture, published my first poem, and gave my first real reading. All three experiences were intimidating and powerful.

This period of my life also brought me closer to my Palestinian roots and helped me locate and relocate myself as a person and a writer among Arabs. But I never ceased to belong to the American literary scene because I wrote in English, often went back to Boston and New York, and wrote for American journals and magazines. However, the American publishing world was and continues to be daunting, extremely intimidating, and difficult for any writer, let alone a young one. It is so difficult to find a publisher to publish a single poem. In the Arab world, authors subsidize their works, so anyone can publish a book. It was also during that time that I discovered the work of the Arab critic and author Salma Khadra Jayyusi. Her research and anthologies remain invaluable in my opinion. When I edited *The Poetry of Arab Women: A Contemporary Anthology*, I wanted to edit an anthology that was as thorough and well-researched as her own.

After about five years in France, I decided to do my postgraduate degree and was accepted at the University of London. London marked one of the most exciting periods of my life. It was a defining moment for me because I started to find my place in the literary scene and started to carefully listen to the music in my work. Music has always been important to me when I write. I started performing with musicians and did a CD, *Traveling Rooms*, with two Russian musicians.

A few years later, I discovered through other writers the existence of low-residency M.F.A. programs. It became clear to me while writing my thesis for the University of London that I did not want to continue to be diverted from my creative writing life. However, I was already far along in my research, which I wrote on the politics of identity and double consciousness in the narratives of Arab American women poets, so I continued and finished the degree, but I also applied to different M.F.A. programs. Bennington College was my first choice, and I was thrilled to get accepted. I moved back to the United States.

While at Bennington, I not only focused on my writing but I got a very close view of the American literary life. I explored many different writing styles, forms, and themes, the way I explored all the countries I traveled to, lived in, and belonged to. At Bennington, I also became aware of how important it was to have done the critical writing and research I had. I was extremely grateful to have studied at the University of London. It gave me a strong base and formation, allowing me to think critically, gain research and reading skills, gain knowledge and confidence.

During that time, I started (re)thinking identity. It had been too heavy a topic in my life for me not to come to some resolve with it. Those who have not been exiled or who have not lost their country might not understand to what degree identity can be haunting. Indeed, it is rich to have traveled and lived the world but we long to belong, we need to know that the trees of our country are growing inside of us. We need to understand our dislocation and expulsion, our attachment and detachment, our exile and condition. We need to understand the questions we ask, the obvious ones and those we might not have otherwise asked. We need to understand the questions: Where are you from? What are you? And understand why these questions are important to answer. We need to understand why others might not see us the way we see ourselves; accept to some degree another's perception of us even if it might not be the way we perceive ourselves for it is a definition that belongs to them.

Identity came knocking at my door again when the author Ethelbert Miller told me that I had to define myself as a writer—was I Palestinian

American, Arab American, French, Dominican (by then my parents had been living in the Dominican Republic for many years)? How do you know where you belong as a writer when you do not belong anywhere? And hyphenation is an American tradition, and a new definition I added to my list of definitions. But must we define ourselves so rigidly?

I was born in fragments and obliged to define myself within borders others drew or defined. It is through writing that I have found a certain kind of wholeness and have been able to say I am French, Palestinian, American, Latina. I am a writer. I often accentuate a different part of my identity according to where I am and who I am with. Andre Aciman has written that an exile is someone who has not only lost his home but who cannot find another, so he reinvents home with what he has, the way we reinvent love with what's left of it. I keep reinventing my identity, my homes. At this juncture, I have found my country in words, and know that worlds there are many, we simply do not search for them, keep looking in the same places.

I graduated from Bennington and went to New York. It was there that everything in my life up until then came together. I found all the accents in my poems in the city's voices, screams, whispers.

I have learned that the possibilities are never ending. I have always thought that a poem is a miracle, that words are gods. Words and their infinite character and power have not ceased to seduce me and take me beyond the journey. I want to write everything as to not forget anything. I want to write time, even if time rewrites itself too often and too frequently for me to ever stay long enough in it, for me to see it and see myself in it. I finish this essay before I am ready to, and it is too early for morning. I am ahead of the day, ahead of myself, ahead of my words, and keep finding out about it afterward.

To live in a house of words, see the world as words, understand the self, the homeland through words, die with bones turned words, is the writer that I am. And how sad to leave this earth never really knowing any country the way a countrywoman should know her country—its every song, silence of morning, echoes of night, its scars and secrets, the way it makes love and seduces, its every turn. And how fortunate it is to leave this earth really knowing the country in each word, and coming home to these lines finally and again.

Poems

El Almuerzo de Tia Habiba

It is only half past six in the morning
and the kitchen is wide awake,

no time for many cups of café on Fridays
for Tia Liliana, Tia Mercedes,
Tia Rosette, Tia Esperanza,
Tia Josephina, Tia Margareta,
Tia Layla and Tio Wadie
come for some of Tia Habiba's
tamalitos, lamb, hummos, laban, and grape leaves.
"Dios mio niña, you are not dressed," Juanita tells me.
Her Indian features recite poems her ancestors told her
the way Tia Habiba's deep curved eyes
tell me about the holy land.
"Por favor, it is not morning yet," I respond.
These are what my Friday mornings
are like when I visit relatives in Torreon, Coahuila,
a little ciudad in Mexico.

By noontime, everyone has arrived,
voices crowd every room.
Before I go downstairs, I stand
at the top of the staircase looking
at those people below as if I was
on the Mount of Olives looking
at the Old City, and I wonder
how these people got here,
so far from the Mediterranean sea,
the desert heat, now they are caught
between Abdel Halim Hafez and Luis Miguel,
jelabas and sombreros, lost in the smoke
coming from the *arguileh*.
I start going down the stairs, hear
them say, *Habibti, que tal?*
And know that all has changed.

In Search of Midnight

He kissed my lips at midnight
I let him
He took my blouse off
I let him
Took my bra off
and touched my breast
I let him

He took my pants off
I let him
Took my underwear off
and looked at me standing
in this strange, dark
black and white room
. . . I let him
A small light dimmed
by the window
I took a glimpse of
the city we live in,
both do not know . . .
Then he pronounces
my name wrong
and I stop him . . .
Ask him if he has ever
been exiled or imprisoned
if he has ever mailed
letters to a woman he
once loved but would
never see again
if he thinks we can go back
to a lover even if
we might not love
the second time,
asked him if he ever
robbed a small grocery store
or stole a bread from a peasant,
if he has ever crossed
seas, coasts and mountains
and still could
not arrive wherever one
thinks one should . . .

He looked at me and said:
I did not pronounce my name
correctly in my country
so I was tortured,
I did not pronounce my name
correctly at the enemy line
so I was exiled
I did not pronounce my name
correctly upon arrival here

so I was given new papers . . .
You see—a heart in search of midnight
is only a heart in search of midnight,
everything else is the same
except what the other is expecting . . .

Detained

For Mourad and all those unjustly detained
in Palestine and elsewhere, and to Ghassan

Over a cup of Arabic coffee
back in nineteen ninety nine,
on a balcony in Ramallah,
we spoke of the *situation*,
how we survive, *we don't you said.*

We had more coffee
your hand trembled
your trembling revealing
your fears the years
you never saw go by
the wait jailing you
your wife and child . . .

Three years later
you are detained . . .
I imagine a cell as tall as you—
five foot eleven inches,
as wide as you—
twenty-one and a half inches,
your life reduced to your body
and your memory of light,
your wife's whispers slide
under the slim opening of
the iron door to remind you
that you must not forget these hours
who you were, are—
we forget too easily
keep changing back to ourselves . . .

But brother, don't be jealous
of another's memories,
don't be jealous of your memories,
just remember what they
have done to themselves—
that the darkness they have planted
in our bones will cripple their bones,
that detainment is their life sentence,
that their blood staining our graves
is a stubborn witness.

The Conflict

They came as if I was not there—
thirty-three, one hundred and twenty-five
long hair, brown hair, blue eyes
lines on the sides of my mouth
yellow skin.

They came while I was out buying bread,
not knowing that I walk
outside the house
without myself

It was not morning yet—
two ambulances, three fire trucks,
twenty-four cars passed in eighty-two seconds,
and they came.

They came with death on their uniforms,
perhaps we are not meant to understand everything,
so we try to understand everything else—
where we are from, where we are going,
what we look like . . .

They came with a picture of a subway ticket
and half a bottle of juice,
told me I could leave,
as if I needed their permission
as if I was in the wrong place,
told me I won't shiver when I sleep
or dream of moist earth anymore,

as if they knew my every thought,
told me I don't need to follow
misery at ever corner of these streets,
don't need to see my sidewalks bleeding anymore,
as if that would change my mind . . .

They came to tell me that
I do not understand the place I inherited
so they will help me leave,
and I realize—we are far from each other,
and grow farther still, smaller still
like broken glass shattered in our throats,
our breathes abandoning God.

Politics

The Itinerary of an Arab American Writer

Etel Adnan

Introduction

It is difficult to underestimate the impact of Etel Adnan's work for the genre of Arab American literature. Born in 1925 in Beirut, Lebanon, Adnan lived in France while studying philosophy at the Sorbonne in Paris. Later she came to the United States and pursued her studies at the University of California–Berkeley, and at Harvard University.

Adnan taught philosophy at Dominican College in San Rafael, California, from 1958 to 1972. In 1972, she returned to Lebanon, where she was the cultural editor of a newspaper, *Al-Safa*. She returned to the United States after seven years, where she wrote the scripts of two documentaries of the Lebanese war. The anti-war theme is a common thread that runs strongly through her work.

Adnan's life is marked by a common postcolonial crisis: though she was raised in an Arabic-speaking country, she was unable to master the language because her schooling was in French and English. Consequently, she writes in English and French, but not in Arabic. At one point in her life, her frustration at being unable to express herself completely in Arabic caused her to turn to painting, which allowed her to express herself without the use of words. She currently creates art in a variety of media, including oils, ceramics, and tapestry.

Her first book was a collection of poetry, *From A to Z* (1982), followed three years later by *The Indian Never Had a Horse and Other Poems* (1985). Her most influential work by far is *Sitt Marie Rose*, a novel published in 1982. Winner of the France-Pays Arabes award in Paris, *Sitt Marie Rose* tells the story of a young Christian woman in Beirut who is brutally murdered—an embodiment of the way that the Lebanese civil war destroyed the beauty and spirit of the city itself. The novel has been celebrated as a powerful testament of the inhumanity of war. Translated into six languages, *Sitt Marie Rose* is a classic in the genres of Arab and Arab American literatre and is part of the curriculum of many literature, Middle Eastern, postcolonial studies, and women's studies courses in universities around the world.

Adnan divides her time between Lebanon, France, and California, and continues to actively create art and write.

I think that I started to write between the ages of seven and eight. As I grew up in Beirut, Lebanon, I went to the neighborhood school run by French nuns. As I was an only child, I liked school: it meant meeting other children. It also meant playing with children. My favorite time was recreation breaks in the squarish "garden" of the school. That large area, at least it seemed to be large, had a fountain in its middle and some trees around the fence. It was fenced with green painted bars the height of a child. It was an enclosure, it was well defined, and that must have impressed me. In kindergarten, we had books. From my early days in life, I identified books with seriousness, not fun. We did not have "children's books" that time in that city. Probably not around the whole Mediterranean.

Although my father was a highly educated person, having gone to the Ottoman Military Academy in Istanbul, and having been a general staff officer during World War I, there were very few books in our house. I remember very distinctly a Koran, and one beaten-down Turkish–German dictionary. A few other books are lost in my memory. In my aunt's house in Damascus, there were some books too, but when I saw her read, it was the Koran that she read, although I often heard my father say that she knew it by heart, like he himself did.

My father often read the local Arab press; while in Damascus, his native city, he read a newspaper there. In Damascus, they were discussing "politics" all the time. My mother was a Greek from Smyrna, Turkey. When she was born, the city was a predominantly Greek city. It's there that my parents were married as my father, at the end of the war, was the military commander of Smyrna. My mother came from a family of artisans and had a limited formal education. She could read Greek and also some French. The language my parents had in common was Turkish. So I grew up speaking Greek and Turkish until I went to the French school.

My mother had, in her room, a little shelf in one of the corners on which she had a few icons. In front of the icons, she had a little oil lamp that was regularly lit in the night, like in Greek churches. On that shelf, she had the Gospels in Greek, and next to them my father's little Koran. For her, sacred books went together.

She used to, at a certain time, when her niece came to visit, read novels in Greek in a loud voice with her niece listening attentively and me intermittently. I remember the stories told and retold in these historical novels full of adventures, the life of Cleopatra, a novel called *Thelma*, and a biography of St. Mary the Egyptian—all read with the same interest and, I am sure, with the sense that all stories somehow belong to the same world.

I became a writer before becoming a reader. In the French system of education, and certainly during the days when I was growing up, there was much emphasis on reading and writing, reading school books correctly, and expressing myself on paper. That approach consisted of daily classes in the study of grammar and classes in composition. As I don't remember with great accuracy the years involved for particular studies, I would think that around the time we were seven years old, we had *rédaction*, a term meaning creating sentences around words chosen by the teacher. It went like this: "Write a line or two using the word 'chair'" or any other word that was given. I remember very clearly, almost as I were back in those moments, that I wrote very often, not a few lines, but long sentences and paragraphs made of these words, and what's remarkable is that I remember the intense involvement I had with writing the sentences; it was a kind of serious happiness that I always experience in those moments, very close to what I still feel when I write. My paragraphs must have been beautiful, as the teacher often read them as examples to the class. Sometimes I used to write the homework of some of my little friends, and they would get good grades, and I would have lesser grades because, I suppose, my imagination was exhausted and my own "compositions," coming last, were uninteresting!

Later, when I was fourteen or fifteen, my classmates and I were asked to write stories. The subject matter used to be given to the whole class, and we had to build up some story around it. Some of these assignments had to be completed in class; others were homework and had to be written at home. Two incidents around these projects are traumatic and have never left my memory.

The first one had to do with homework. I do not remember the subject of the homework, but I know that I wrote it dutifully and submitted it in the morning. The next day I was severely scolded by the teacher. She furiously accused me of having presented a work written by my parents: I denied it, of course, and that made her more adamant. I was (thankfully) too young, too much of a child, to take the whole scene as a compliment.

A year or so after that incident, we had an examination, and examinations were always solemn affairs (like everything else in a religious school). We were supposed to write a composition "with a moral attached to it." As adolescents, we had to do such assignments more or less regularly. I invented a story where two kids in a field trespassed a fence and walked on the grass for some time until the owner of the property came to reprimand them; as one of the kids wore a hat and as they were supposed to behave in a morally correct way, I made them use very polite, flowery language, and made the elder take his hat off and bow. Somehow, I remember the flow of the story, its rhythm, its smoothness, and it was in fact singled out, read aloud by the teacher as an example of a good "composition." I was quite happy. At 4:00 P.M., the hour that classes are disbanded, the nun who had congratulated me in public took me aside and said something along these lines: "You could certainly not have written this work. You must have read it somewhere and learned it by heart." I insisted that it was not the case, knowing, to start with, that we had no French books at home, and the school was not lending books. All we had were textbooks that the school was itself selling. Still, that nun looked at me with the face she had in catechism when speaking of sins and sinners, as if to say that I was a liar, even a very shrewd one.

The stories I just evoked show that already as children we were doing "creative writing" with no self-consciousness, like we were painting without calling it art.

Following the baccalaureate exams, I went to the Ecole Supérieure des Lettres, the equivalent of a French department in a university, but the Ecole, in those years that followed World War II, was an independent institute. It was in these enchanting years that I ran into poets such as Baudelaire, Rimbaud, Gerard de Nerval, and Mallarmé. These courses were in preparation for the License des Lettres. We were relatively few students, and that created a sense of belonging to a privileged group, to an almost mystic alliance around poetry. Poetry had instantly become a world that we joined, like one joins a secret society, and our allegiance was total. We were about twenty students, as the Ecole had just opened, and we had the luck to have a teacher who was a "master," a man named Gabriel Bounoure, who was also one of the most prestigious critics of French poetry and literature in his time.

We were not involved in a grade system, as it didn't exist at the college level. We were not judged. We were not competitive. So the spirit of poetry was able to penetrate us in all innocence. I still believe, half a century later, that poetry and spiritual freedoms go together. We lived under a spell. Poetry still has that power on my mind. It instantly creates its own world and its own rules and its own integrity.

We had no assignments, only a final examination. We were not taught "writing." We read the poets and attended open-ended master classes during which Bounours was following the course of his thinking, sometimes dialoguing with us, sometimes almost daydreaming while we sat oblivious of the hour.

Although the purpose of the class was to teach French poetry, the teacher also mentioned German literature, the great German Romantic movement, Novalis, and Rilke. I can swear, without lying, that I befriended Rilke in those days, although of course I didn't, but so involved were we with him that he mingles with memories of "real life" to this day.

For a long time, I didn't see myself as a poet, or a writer, and certainly not in those days. We had such a reverence for poets and writers that we thought that no one ever said that he or she was one. It was up to the others, and in relation to the best ones, to say who was a poet. And I am still shocked, even if I am ready to admit that I am wrong in so doing, when I hear some person who has written a handful of poems declare himself or herself a poet. I am always reticent to say that I am one, for many reasons, one of them being that it is not up to me to decide.

I started when I was twenty or twenty-one to write something that I considered to eventually become a poem. (Here, I have to say that it has been easy for me to say that I wrote poetry, but not that I was a poet. That's all there is to it.) From elementary school on, French became my main language, my main tool of expression. I insist on the word *tool*, because it was not my mother tongue. My mother tongue(s) were to remain oral, since I never learned them in schools.

As the French schools in Lebanon neglected the local Arabic culture, and as I belonged to the generation that went to school before London's independence, I did not learn Arabic at all, save the "street" Arabic, the most basic words that one uses in small transactions. This, I came to regret all my life, although in the United States I took in Arabic summer classes that improved my Arabic but never allowed me to write in what should have been my natural language.

Being as steeped in French culture as I had become made me mentally a French person, although instinctively I always resented the colonial system that alienated, gradually, the majority of the educated Lebanese from their own past, their cultural identity and the larger environment of the Arab world. Such a colonial legacy is almost never overcome.

And so I wrote my own poem: since my early childhood, I went swimming. Little girls in the early thirties were not used to be taken to swim, so I felt very special and also developed a passion for the sea that I still have. The title of my long poem was "Le Livre de la Mer" (The Book of the Sea). I perceived the relations between the sun and the sea, both omnipresent in Beirut, as a cosmic marriage. And these words being gendered in French, I saw the masculine sun married to the feminine sea. This was the core of the poem.

It wasn't yet finished when I received a scholarship to continue my studies in Paris. Studying philosophy at the Sorbonne, I continued to write poetry occasionally. I was absolutely not moved by theories and would write poems, it seemed, in moments of crisis. The themes that recurred, I noticed later, were those of a cosmic awareness and of the discovery of the tragic situations that love can bring about. Love for the universe and love in the sense of passion remained, I can say, the energy that sustained my writings all through my life. Later, when I came to the United States as a graduate student at Berkeley, California, a third passion took hold of me, a historical and political passion for the Arab world.

When I arrived at Berkeley in January 1955, I had no preconceptions of America and the discovery of this continent was a continuous shock. Most importantly, and certainly in the first years, it was the American language itself that kept my attention.

I realized how poor my English was when I arrived and the difficulty was compounded by the philosophy department's offered courses: these were centered around linguistics, symbolic logic, and the philosophy of science. A new aspect of philosophy was unfolding and that was fascinating, but it obliged me to make efforts on many fronts. I then spent a year at Harvard and learned to appreciate the intellectual history of the United States. Among other things, I was surprised to find out how much religion had shaped the thinking of the early makers of America.

Being immersed in my daily life (and problems), I was not involved in writing but rather in the discovery of a new world: these were times when I was as thrilled by jazz music as by American football, by the deserts in America as by its oceans, and interested by the plight of the American Indian and by the spirit of democracy. The complexities of America need more than a lifetime to be understood.

Speaking in English was an adventure, but it also resolved my ambiguous relation to the French language: something deep inside me has always been resentful of the fact that French came to us in Lebanon through a colonial occupation, that it was imposed, that it was not innocently taught me as a second language, but a language meant to replace Arabic. For me, English had no such connotations. It was also a language freer in its structure than French (which has, of course, its own beauty). I realized, through using it, how much the very use of language is a creative process.

I must say that when I landed in the United States, I had a kind of fluid identity: was I Greek, Ottoman Arab, almost French? Was I just a human being living on this planet (not an unpleasant feeling)? At least I didn't feel like an exile, as I chose to come, and encountered an open and dynamic society, or rather a whole new world.

It was in Berkeley that all the threads that made up my mind and my soul came together: I became what I was, I became an Arab, at the same time that I was becoming an American. It is there that I met students from all over the Arab world, while I was familiar only with people from Lebanon and Syria. This world became a reality, in all its interplay of local identities and transnational solidarity.

At Berkeley, I also met the first Palestinians I ever saw and the close contact with their personal history changed my life. Palestine was not anymore some problem I was hearing about, but a real neighbor to Lebanon that was dramatically destroyed by an oncoming wave of European Jews settling on territories that belonged for centuries and centuries to the indigenous people.

Many things happened then, simultaneously: the discovery of a historically tragic event concerning all the Arabs (as we have seen it since), a shame of now knowing it before, and an anger at the injustice inflicted upon people, who, to make things worse, were demonized by the American press. They had to be demonized in order to justify the cultural and then, progressively, physical genocide to which they were submitted. Palestine then became a continuous thread in most of my poetry and writing.

Probably because of the switch from French to English, I was not writing for many years. When I ended up teaching philosophy at Dominican College in San Rafael, California, I became involved in American life and American issues. I also became a painter. Painting was a joy, the happiest of occupations, and an expression that bypasses spoken language. I was at peace with it.

The Vietnam War was my first confrontation with the realities, the details, of war. I was heartbroken by the sight of Vietnamese peasants being burned alive when their huts were set on fire, by the wounded and killed, including young American soldiers sent to duty into a hellish situation.

I started receiving some literary magazines, containing some antiwar poetry, in the faculty room of the college. One evening, after the six o'clock news, I sat naturally in front of my little, old portable typewriter, and wrote a poem whose title I wanted to be ironic. It was "The Ballad of the Lonely Knight in Present Day America," and it was a series of two-line stanzas. I sent it to the *S.B. Gazette*, a local two-page, newspaper-format literary magazine devoted entirely to the antiwar movement. I got a reply, quick, enthusiastic, and informal. The whole thing was enchanting, since I was, and still am, attracted to open, informal approaches to things, and certainly to the various ways of human expression.

The publication of that poem made me an Arab American poet. I mean that, with it, I entered the mainstream of the American antiwar movement and the community of its poets. It was followed by other poems in the same vein and created contacts with a whole network of poets and artists across the United States. I felt integrated.

Strangely enough, these poems also linked me to my French education. In my adolescent years, I was not only passionately interested in Baudelaire and Rimbaud but also with the French poets of the Resistance, such as Louis Aragon, Paul Éluard, Pierre-Jean Jouve. Soon after, because of the 1967 war, I felt myself part of another resistance, the one organized by the Palestinians. It was resistance elsewhere than in Europe, but the principles were the same: a lyrical, cultural opposition to oppression, to the dehumanizing forces in the world that take on many disguises. I felt strongly that there was such a thing as transnational desires to resist and to become part of an open and generous movement in favor of those that Frantz Fanon named "the wretched of the world." And it was poetic justice that my first poem concerning Palestine and titled "Jebu" (a reference to the Jebusites, the original Canaanite founders of Jerusalem) was first published neither in the United States nor in Lebanon, but in Rabat, Morocco, in the magazine *Souffles*, published by Abdellatif Laabi for his own fight against injustices in his own country. To fight against oppression automatically breaks the tribal bonds of an individual and creates new open links with the world.

By becoming, through my various activities and singularly through my activities as a painter and a writer, an Arab American who integrated as much as possible the trajectory of her life, I think that I also speak in my writings and other endeavors for a community with which I share a tremendous historical and cultural heritage, common values with the best of the American experience, and hopes for more justice for the Arabs and for others.

Poem

Following are excerpts from *There: In the Light and the Darkness of the Self and the Other*.

Reprinted with permission of Post-Apollo Press.

THERE

And there sat our shadows facing each other, and were you behind the veil, the wall? Your eyes were absorbing the blueness of sorrow while I was looking at the Nile, the river starting in the horizon, coming down large terraces, frenzied, frightening, and a flower reached me, ate at my substance, became a butterfly goddess, and we went on, into a trance.

Can't we understand each other and stop the killing, without the dance, the run and the walk?

This morning? It's too early for the beach, too soon for starting a fight, so we linger on some light beam and go through windows, unnoticed, while the Police is waiting with sticks, gloves, gases, orders to shoot or not to shoot beyond one's brain, but can the Police stay calm anymore than a flower from the Nile can stop rising from the water and become a parachute, a World War II celestial machine which has already left for outer space? We're weak, sitting, facing each other, antlers locked in battle.

And I sat on the floor, O Shahrazade, with no king to do the listening, no beggar, and are you there, behind the curtains, beyond our mountains?!

Who is my enemy, and should I have one, is he my former friend, was he young when he came to slaughter, did he, mistakenly, shoot down his daughter?

The sun is above me, the original one that angels speak about, a ball of fire, look! There's dust over there, storms, there's love, which live, what for, there's SOMETHING over there which keeps growing. . .

It's cold, over there, under primitive tents made of skins as soft as my heart's. You're so beautiful, young fellow, my eyes can't see you, so pale that your presence lights my house.

Look at us, although we don't know to whom we're speaking, you don't have to know me, when the wind blows it brings home your ephemeral beauty, before it's too late, and before we go on similar and different roads to where my mind will be racing faster than my thoughts.

Anyway, who are you? Born under a female sign, a warrior, woman or man, and does it matter when desire rises before we know it, telling things unknown?

You stand in front of me like death, or the last Word, made of time, speed . . . You deported live flesh, made curses come to life and melt within our bones. Who can I call a friend?

Always, on the pleated horizon, there's fear, and some instability runs like a god of earlier days, or the first thought-wave, and I'm in a hurry, aren't you too, you whom I can't call woman or man?

Are you transparent water like my eyes used to be, do I have the last word on this? Are you the Beast of the Apocalypse, needing a corn field for your wedding, your wedding? . . .

They're shooting on the frontline, shaking the kids out of their sleep, as it happened already, over there, when nobody watches.

You live in the soul's darkness, somewhere in Southern Spain, where we were married, and divorced, where you got sick-leave, the Church looking down over our shoulders, when it was not crucifying us or burning our books.

Why do you bother with yesteryears now that we're going to the moon with rockets, beyond Mercury although not beyond our miseries, why grief, salt water, hunger?

The system is cracking, it's an implosion, the debris are human limbs, who cares?

You're facing me, aren't you, or you might not be there and I may have to go to the movies, where half of us go, the other half going to hell. But beware. Roles are interchangeable, and you keep sending me messages care of pelicans.

In this afternoon, this ominous moment, what answers do you have, what clash of wills are we fostering when we answer a bullet with a bullet, a thousand corpses with as many corpses? Who should feed the wolves?

[. . . .]

THERE

Such impotence in so much beauty, there . . . Why are there so many prostitutes among the men; street corners, garbage, police and flies feeding on corpses, heat, narrowness?

Don't bargain for my possessions. They may not disappear. Here, around the house, defined perimeters keep the sea's roar away from my head. You're hiding behind rose bushes. I'm sweating each night, your face confronting me with its perennial presence.

Women weep under their black robes, they climb and throw flowers and rice instead of grenades, do listen, do you exchange arguments with me or with them, why is the sea green when we're talking, remembering my grandparents whom I never met—their dust was already spread over the highlands when I was born—and you keep asking if I'm still alive and I have no answer to that.

Currents meet in my body while it swims and I become water, part of water. The "you" is always the "I" so we inhabit each other in our irremediable singleness.

Deep in my sleep, water was running and there's war said your voice, the future was being dismantled, and is love possible, your question hangs over my tranquility.

Yes, whose and whose beginning, comets are exploding on the side of wounded planets. Space is black-and-white movies, and your skin is catching fire.

Who is eating at the mountain when the moon sits on it? Before memory came into being there was an orange moon, there, and I went by it, walking, passenger of its sister-planet, and we were alone and why I don't know.

This heat is keeping the pressure on us, something will break loose in this speed, this terror.

[. . . .]

THERE

In this my place time is shut off, death could be a beginning, a revolution's starting point: in the stillness surrounded by the highest trees, then the mountains, and beyond, the left-overs of History. . .

Here, I carry my *hereness* with my luggage; your body is decaying statue, forget Italy, its poisonous hillsides, let's cross that bridge before the falling of autumn's leaves.

You can, if you desire, sweep your floor with my family's parchments, but beware, the wind is rising, the air becoming metal. I live in a luminosity which renews its vigor.

There stands a tree. You're pushing the desert onward. With my legs folded under me I'm sitting, where? on the edge; over here, a sea of dust.

Deeper the oblivion deeper the hauntedness. We built unmeasurable empires. The horses, though, wanted the fields to be bordered fearing the salt mines.

Is there a language for lovers which doesn't need the lovers? Should we exchange genealogies over a poet's sealed body?

Do we have a land? Are the balconies ours, did we dangle our legs over the balustrade, were you a child with curling hair and me, impatient to grow?

We do worship the waves, don't we? Strange birds are chased away, I presume by the tribe. While battles rage, when long memory lines wait to be revived, the slaughter of shepherds goes on and death becomes a moving shadow on a screen.

I become a voracious animal, searching for self-affirmation on corpses—metaphorical for you and me—but real to those who left behind such decomposed traces.

HERE

What is here?: a place or an idea, a circle focused in God's eye, a cosmic wave's frozen frame, transient, doomed?

Here, where the heat mollifies, when the body surrenders before solicitations could reach it, and there, where the temperature boils the mind and makes it explode into sudden action; here is the point of no return . . .

[. . . .]

THERE

Enmity made us lovers, and you died of it, there, on the line, between ocean and sand. In that night you met your darkest encounter. An overdose of happiness kills as surely as lightening [*sic*].

There, a procession of fires proceeded towards the forest. It needed additional fuel to feed its passion. Is destruction an inseparable component of love?

On my American screen I saw the Vietnamese peasant who was running and on whose skin napalm on fire was closer than his wife: war, which liberates and kills those it liberated, joined us forever.

On Becoming a Writer

Ghada Karmi

Introduction

Ghada Karmi is a leading Palestinian activist, academic and writer. She is currently a research fellow at the Institute of Arab and Islamic Studies at the University of Exeter, England. She is also vice-chair of the Council for the Advancement of Arab-British Understanding. Her previous posts included The Royal Institute of International Affairs and the School of Oriental and African Studies, both in London.

Born in Jerusalem, she left with her family to England in 1948, the year Israel was established and the first Arab–Israeli war ensued. She was raised and educated in England, where she qualified in medicine from Bristol University and later acquired a doctorate in the history of Arabic medicine from London University. Her memoir, *In Search of Fatima: A Palestinian Story* (2002), recounts her memories of Palestine and her family's struggles during the diaspora. The memoir has been praised for its originality and style, as well as for its depiction of the Palestinian refugee crisis.

Karmi has been involved in political lobbying for thirty years for the cause of Palestinian national independence, and she has appeared often on British television and radio. Her articles and essays have appeared in numerous publications, including the British newspaper *The Guardian*. In addition to *In Search of Fatima*, she has also edited two books: *Jerusalem Today: What Future for the Peace Process?* (2000) and *The Palestinian Exodus: 1948–1998* (2000).

I had always wanted to be a writer. As a child, growing up in England in a household with a literary father, I would go around making up stories and recounting them with great relish to whichever unfortunate child or adult I could collar into listening to me. I would sometimes write down these stories, in a style usually copied from whatever novel I happened to be reading at the time. These compositions were gauche, pretentious, and highly fanciful. I was an avid reader and had read most of the major English and French classics by the age of thirteen. As a teenager I decided I would study literature or history at university to underpin my literary leanings. I daydreamed of joining the literati of my day, was so in love with famous writers that I used to wish I had lived at the time of Charles Dickens, to imagine the thrill of having been contemporary with him or with George Eliot or Jane Austen. The world their novels created for me was more vivid and more real than my own.

This was the more remarkable, given my origins. I was no English child, reared on English apprehensions and sensibilities; indeed, nothing could have been more inimical to the culture into which I was born. The idea of anyone enjoying William Makepeace Thackeray or Honoré de Balzac in my town of origin, Tulkarm in Palestine, would have been bizarre. In fact I was born in Jerusalem but my father's family originated from this place, which is now part of the so-called West Bank and an area of bitter conflict. By the time of my birth, the family had moved to Jerusalem, where I spent my first eight years. At the point of our forced departure from it in 1948 as the state of Israel was being established, I had just managed to read and write Arabic with reasonable proficiency and to learn just two words of English, Oscar Wilde. This was because one of the books in my father's library bore his name and I had learned to decipher the letters of the English alphabet. Otherwise, I knew no English and when we arrived, bewildered and displaced, in London, it was to find an alien world that I had to face without language or previous experience.

Growing up in the England of the time was a daunting experience for my mother too. She was no better equipped to deal with her new environment than I or my brother and sister were. So she resolved her difficulties by simply re-creating the lost world of Jerusalem and the Arab society and culture that she knew in the heart of London. As a result, we grew up in as Arab an environment as she could make it, and our interaction with the England around us became no more than daily forays into a foreign land. It was in this strange dichotomous world that I first developed my taste for English literature. Early on, I learned to escape from the stifling shackles of my rigidly Arab home into a magical otherworld where there was no conflict of culture. As the divergence between this home life and the English context wherein it was incongruously set grew and became translated into a crisis of identity for me, I took refuge with ever greater devotion in the seemingly uncomplicated, English side. Within a few years, I could not have been more identified with England than if I had been English-born and bred for generations.

At the age of sixteen, I announced my intention of pursuing an arts education that would be the prelude to my writing career. But to my dismay, I came up against unexpected opposition. I discovered that my father had quite other plans for me. His chief concern, he said, was that I acquire a trade that would give me independence and a steady income, a skill that I could carry with me wherever I went. Having been forced out once from our home, who knew if it could happen again? And if it did, how would we survive? Far better to be a doctor or an engineer (my brother's profession) with a transferable skill than a (useless) writer or historian. This was how he reasoned and, much against my will, I was diverted into the science stream at school, in preparation for a career in medicine. I wept in frustration at this decree, but felt powerless to oppose it. I duly completed my examinations for university entrance and became a medical student at Bristol University, in the west of England.

Six frustrating years later, I qualified, having endured the stifling of my ambitions and the company of my medical colleagues, whom I found unspeakably dull, limiting and unimaginative. But it was too late, I thought, as I worked the long hours of a doctor in training and, later, of a hospital specialist. It took me years to have the courage to throw off the medical yoke and turn my hand to something more akin to my natural inclinations. With the burden of a medical degree and the need to earn my living round my neck, I saw that it would take great ingenuity to reshape my career along the lines of something so different as literary writing. Eventually an opportunity presented itself in a field that combined both medicine and literature: medical history. This was, at the time, a respectable occupation for retired doctors and professional historians who, it was said, had not made it in the "straight" history field. I was neither, but I somehow managed to convince the history of medicine institute in London I approached of the unique contribution I could make.

Quite simply, I proposed studying the history of medieval Arabic, often called "Islamic," medicine. The combination of medical and linguistic skills that I commanded qualified me uniquely to pursue this subject, I said. It worked and I received a handsome grant that maintained me in reasonable style for the next six years. My underlying agenda was not, of course, to study medical history at all, but the chance it would give me to make my escape from medical servitude forever, as I then hoped, and turn my hand to proper writing. This for me meant creative, narrative writing, the sort that novelists use. At the same time, I had enough decency to recognize that I would have to fulfil, my obligations to the institute, tedious as these would be. But I believed this could be fitted into my secret program without great hardship.

As I began my studies, I found to my surprise that what had started out as a ruse to enable an orderly transition from medicine to literature in fact had a life and fascination of its own. I learned that, unlike their modern counterparts, the doctors of medieval society were polymaths who could combine knowledge of philosophy, geography, astronomy, and even poetry, in some cases, with medicine. Their books, many of which survive only in manuscript form and which I perused with avid curiosity, opened a window, not as I had thought merely on an obsolete medical system, but on the workings of a whole society whose norms and customs are beyond our reach. I learned that the medieval doctors considered love a brain disease with specific signs, symptoms, and a range of treatments; that slaves for sale in the marketplace were subject to a medical examination to assess their fitness for joining the family where they would work, not as servants but almost as adopted children; that the science of cosmetics was well advanced; that wine was widely prescribed as therapy in what were Islamic societies; that regular sexual intercourse was considered essential for normal health and strongly recommended for "medicinal purposes"; and many other things besides.

A wealth of material was clearly here for narrative literature. But, constrained as I was by a scientific training that favored note taking and abbreviations over prose, coupled with the arid, scholastic style beloved of the traditional medical historians I was reading, I made little headway. In a short time, I learned to write in the same stuffy style as the historians I was trying to emulate. I thought about writing a book on Arabic medicine but allowed myself to be persuaded to study for a doctorate instead. I would improve my chances of acquiring an academic post, the argument went. The research and reading of obscure texts this involved ensured that I remained locked into the academic mode. This culminated in a doctoral thesis so dry and scholastic it could compete with the best of my classical sources. For my pains, I was awarded a Ph.D. from London University and three bound copies of my thesis that are still on my shelf gathering dust.

Even so, during the years it took for me to attain this, I tried to write a novel for a competition on Palestine. I did not win, and what little confidence I had in my literary abilities evaporated. Worse still, someone at the institute found out about it and complaints were made to the trust that had awarded me my grant that their money was being diverted into "PLO projects." (This was the 1970s, following the first Palestinian hijackings and the Munich Olympics attack, and the Palestine Liberation Organization was seen by many in Britain as an outlaw or terrorist organization). Whether this incident contributed to my failure to attain a post in medical history in England thereafter is a moot point. The fact was that by the end of the 1970s, I was no nearer to being the kind of writer I had always aspired to be and the project I had initiated to transform my career in that direction had not succeeded.

For the next ten years I wrote articles and papers on history, but also increasingly on the politics of the Palestinian–Israeli conflict. I had by then become an activist for the Palestine cause and was heavily involved in lobbying and political organization. The professional training I had received was clearly reflected in my writing style. I did not dare try my hand at literature, which was still the only genre I recognized as real writing. I was crushed by the knowledge that I had had no formal literary education or training in writing skills to qualify me to be a writer. So I confined my efforts to "serious" compositions about the subjects I knew and was able to publish several books of this kind, most of them edited rather than written by me. I acquired a reasonable reputation for my expertise and was increasingly regarded as a specialist in the international relations field. The title of "Dr." before my name was taken as denoting a doctorate in this subject; few suspected that its original provenance had been medicine.

And then one day, as if out of the blue, I sat down and decided I would leave all that behind and write about what it meant to be a Palestinian, not in the conventional way as hitherto, but differently—in a personal, human, literary way. This was to be a memoir, a narrative account of my life and that of my family, how we left our native land and subsequently had to adjust to a new society and a new life as refugees in Britain. I do not remember how I arrived at this decision. It seemed to have pushed itself onto me with imperative force, as if there were nothing else more urgent for me to do, a project that had been kept waiting too long and could no longer be postponed. I did not embark on this as a total novice, for just previously, I had started to write a novel about a doomed relationship between people of different cultures, much of it reflecting my own experience with an unhappy love affair. But it was more a stream of reminiscence than a novel and I never imagined it would ever be completed or get published.

The task now was different, and I set to it with eager relish and not much of a writing plan, beyond the decision to pursue a chronological order that would start with my grandfather and work its way down to me. The literary agent I consulted rejected the first draft out of hand. She told me no one wanted to be given "a lesson in history." When I looked at what I had written, I saw what she meant. Still under the influence of my previous training, I had produced yet again another dry and academic text, lacking the very humanity and emotion that makes narrative literature. I had, indeed, included large tracts of historical detail in a worthy but dull attempt to educate the reader.

So I forced myself to pretend that I was still writing the unfinished love-affair novel, willing myself to write and think differently. By then, I was no longer employed—having for many years been obliged, much against my will, to resume my medical career for financial reasons. I suppose I was in what many writers would regard as an enviable position, with much free time and no financial constraints. I had a beautiful apartment in the New Forest, a marvelous woodland area in the south of England that lent itself to reverie and contemplation. I would leave London and take myself off there to immerse myself in writing. And it was there that the greatest part of the book was completed.

I cannot now recall how I actually wrote some of its sections. Somehow, the prose seemed to flow, once I had got started. By the time I had finished, I felt I had done something really important, not just for myself but for all those who had ever suffered dispossession, exile and a disordered sense of belonging. Most of all, I felt I had conveyed to the English-speaking reader a sense of what the Palestinian tragedy was about and what it had really meant for its victims. For the book was primarily written for a Western readership, reared on stories of Jewish suffering and persecution and usually exposed only to the Israeli version of events. It was situated in England and replete with references to English life in a way that would be familiar mostly to those who were English or who knew England intimately. In doing this, I was constantly aware of the difficulties I would face in getting the book to publication. Unlike the novel, which was a private affair, largely written for myself, I was determined that this book should be read, and by ordinary people.

There is no shortage of books on the Middle East conflict, from all its aspects. But these have mostly been tracts as dry as the history of medicine texts I had so earnestly perused in the 1970s. There is a plethora of studies about Palestinian politics, economics, statistics, and international law, but hardly any that speak about the Palestinians as a human community, their feelings, their little stories, their sufferings. Compare the Jewish case, where hardly a single person remains in ignorance of the Holocaust or the historical suffering of the Jews. That is not, of course, because the story was conveyed through historical analyses of World War II or the statistics of displaced persons' camps, or the details of postwar treaties. Rather, it is because of the rich narrative literature, films, plays, diaries, and memoirs written by Jews and non-Jews, through which the human dimension to that history came alive. By contrast, hardly anything exists to fulfill this function for the Palestinians. The number of Palestinian memoirs or novels written in English is minuscule; one thinks of Said Abu Rish, Edward Said, Fawwaz Turki, and, more recently, Ray Hanania and Raja Shehadeh. The situation is not much better with the rest of the Arts.

This made my enterprise more difficult, partly because I had few precedents to refer to and partly because in Britain, where I live, the Palestinian narrative is unpopular. It is even less so in the United States, where

I hoped to have my book distributed. Zionism has done its work well here, driving out any consideration for the Palestinians for anything other than terrorism. They are routinely presented as either gun-waving terrorists or ranting women in head scarves. This is an oversimplification, of course, and in recent years, there has been greater public sympathy for the Palestinian cause. But it is still widely misunderstood and misreported. Moreover, Palestinians are Arabs and mostly Muslims, and neither of these groups enjoys any better approbation in the West.

I recall once being entertained at the home of an English aristocrat, an earl with a country estate. This was not usual company for me, but I was there by virtue of an acquaintance with his daughter, a woman given to charitable works, among which she ranked support for Palestinian refugees. While we were at lunch, a stiff and formal ceremony, where the conversation was confined to anodyne generalities like the weather and the annual hunt, one of the guests suddenly asked where I came from. When I replied, "Palestine," the earl leaned across and said reassuringly to my interlocutor, "Don't worry. It's not what you think. These Palestinians are smart fellows, nothing like the other Arabs."

So, I found myself writing a book that would challenge many assumptions and stereotypes, would be difficult to publish, and might end in a personal disappointment so devastating as to finish off my aspiring literary career forever. There was also the feminine dimension. Although it was not a woman's book as such and not concerned with women's issues, it was undeniably written by a woman and contained domestic scenes whose details and approach could hardly have come from a masculine pen. I wrote about my mother in her kitchen, our village woman Fatima with her embroidered caftan, the all-female gatherings in our house in Jerusalem where women vented their grievances against their husbands, my early and frustrating attempts to get a boyfriend once I'd left home, and much more.

People advised me repeatedly to inflate this feminine aspect of my narrative, to make it more salacious because Arab women are still thought of in this society as exotic, mysterious, and titillating. Fatima Mernissi's book on life in a Moroccan harem, *Dreams of Trespass,* had just then appeared in English translation, and though this was not salacious, its subject matter appealed to just this kind of taste. There should be more about intimacy and sexual relationships and how Arab men treat women, I was advised. "We want to get under the veil," people said, "to get a close view of women's private lives under Islam." Much as I recognized the publicity value of such material I balked at incorporating more of it in the book than there already was—and much of that inserted under this kind of pressure. It was as if Arab women have no intrinsic interest in themselves; their only value lies in their roles as sexual beings, the more provocative the better.

The book I finally ended up with was a culmination of a lifetime of suppressed longings and aspirations. It expressed not only my thwarted literary ambitions, but also my need to tell the story of an oppressed and silenced community whose narrative was too awkward to fit into the official mythology. Palestinians are the real victims of anti-Semitism, the people on whom have been vented the hatreds and prejudices of Jew and non-Jew alike. There never would have been a Jewish state without Jewish persecution in Europe. And yet it was not Europe that was made to accommodate this project to solve the Jewish problem, but a small, weak, and obscure Middle Eastern country that had had no hand in creating it. And because the people of this land were in the way of the Jewish state, they have been dispersed, hounded, and persecuted ever since for that "crime." What had been an ancient, homogeneous native society was shattered into fragments and converted into a nation of refugees, displaced persons, outlaws, and paupers. Worst of all, their voice was silenced so effectively they could not even tell the world how they had been degraded and destroyed.

In writing *In Search of Fatima* I had a double obligation: as one of that unfortunate nation, I had to be true to them but I also had to be true to myself. Only my readers can judge whether I have succeeded.

Fiction

The following is an excerpt from a novel-in-progress, *The Last Chance*.

You could cut the atmosphere with a knife. It was happening again, the silences, the coldness, the pretended disinterest in each other's affairs, the not knowing when it would be OK again—if ever again. And each time it happened these days, she found herself wondering whether it was finally the end and when she would have to start to contemplate life on her own once more. Each time now, this, which had been unthinkable half a year or even less ago, became more familiar, more inevitable. She never spoke of it to him because she thought it might precipitate the very result she was as yet unprepared for, so she kept it to herself as her own private sorrow.

He had gone away overnight on business. They had rarely been apart in the three years since their relationship started, and she sat at home that evening wondering if he would telephone. He didn't. It was a fine early autumn evening, balmy, almost romantic, such that a surge of exhilaration soared through her which she quickly suppressed. In the past, she would have such feelings perhaps on her way home from work and she would hurry to rush into the house and fling her arms around him and tell him how glad she was that he was in her life. Or sometimes she would want to surprise him with a small present or a sudden suggestion for an outing. But all that had died now. Did he know? Did he notice the change? Strange questions, one would think she would know his reactions by now.

She made herself go through the motions of a normal evening at home, ate without much appetite, read in bed, turned the light out and all the time, somewhere she was thinking about him and hoping he would telephone. Earlier that day, before he left, she had started a conversation about "them." He was so preoccupied with his work, she said, he had no room in his life for a relationship.

"I really think that the only way you can cope—I am not saying it's what you want—is if you're left completely alone, without the slightest request or demand placed on you to do anything over and above your own program." She spoke in superficially reasonable tones, as if she were discussing other people, she even affected a small smile meant to reassure him that she was not about to make a scene. In reality, she was desperate. He shifted in his seat uncomfortably, having come in to have his coffee with her at her request although they both knew that he was in a rush. There was always a moment during such conversations when she awaited his reaction with suspense. He could be apologetic, or patient, but more often he was annoyed. These conversations always had the same form. She would fret about their problems inside herself, would give out what she imagined to be signals of her distress which he invariably failed to pick up, and would end up feeling herself impelled to speak out. He himself never initiated similar conversations and disliked having to respond. And although she knew that, she could not stop herself. She had evolved a variety of techniques for broaching the subject, but whichever way she chose, he always took it as an attack on him and resented her for it. This time was no exception. He didn't immediately respond, and she persisted.

"I mean, I get the impression that your work never ends, I mean there would never come a time when you would say, there that's enough, now let's relax, perhaps go out for a walk or to a film or something like that."

She could see that she'd lost him. He looked uncomfortable, but eventually he said, "You know, I do put in a lot of time into this, you don't realize how much time it takes every day to clear up, wash the bathroom, tidy up." This was an old bone of contention between them. He worked from home, while she went out to an office every day. Although they had a cleaner, she came only once a week, and he usually tidied up in the mornings after she left for work. He often mentioned this fact as if he resented it, and from time to time, she would get angry and insist on running around frenetically in the mornings trying to do everything herself.

"And," he continued, "I really don't think you should complain after all that I did last night. Do you realize that I got to bed at 2 a.m.?" She had been unwell for a couple of days, and they had had some friends over for dinner the evening before. Because she could not have coped, he had shopped, cooked, and cleared up after their guests, thus sparing her the effort.

"Yes, I know that, and I have thanked you over and over again for what you did. I'm talking about something else." She paused. He was looking at the floor. "Look, it's not a question of your doing the house-work, I used to have a daily cleaner to do that. I'm talking about being us, being together, going out for a walk, spending time together." Her voice had become both irritable and plaintive. He got up angrily. "I'm not going to sit here listening to this. In any case, I'm late, and I'd better get going." He walked out of the bedroom and went into his study, slamming the door behind him.

She sat on the bed miserably, wondering for the thousandth time where she or they had gone wrong. He came back into the bedroom and started to pack hurriedly, avoiding her. Without thinking, she got up and threw herself against his chest. "Please, please," she begged, "please don't let's part angrily. You're going away tonight, please don't leave like this."

He paused for a moment and then put his arms around her. "Well, why do you make me so angry? Why don't you notice what I do for you?"

She could have replied, but refrained in her desperation for them to make up.

And now she lay in bed sleepless and wondering what he was think-ing, if he was thinking anything about her at all. He had moved in to live with her a year ago, and, unforeseen by either of them, it had led to the virtual destruction of their relationship. They quarreled frequently, the moments of tranquillity ever shorter and rarer. These days, when they made up, it was somehow always incomplete, as if they merely glossed over the surface while the resentments and misunderstandings rumbled on. She was more prone than he to probe and question, but even she shied away from confronting the depths of their problem. Almost per-versely, he talked of washing up and cleaning bathrooms, while she longed for an arm around her shoulders, a hand on her cheek, a mur-mured compliment.

Why had it come to this between them? She was so involved in it that she could hardly distinguish anymore who or what was to blame, could see no pattern or predict any future. At her suggestion, they had started to see a psychiatrist for counseling, and although she was the one who had wanted this to happen, because she believed that it would mag-ically put their situation to instant rights, she had begun to feel that even this was not working. She herself had received several years of psychotherapy at the hands of the same psychiatrist, Dr Aaronson, and it had helped her sort out much of her unhappiness and uncertainty, to the extent that she became convinced of the value of this sort of therapy for everyone who could afford the time and the cost. At first, he resisted the idea, telling her that it was psychobabble, absurd and artificial. Apart from having considerable doubts about the concepts that lay behind psychotherapy, he profoundly disagreed with the mechanisms it employed; it was simply unnatural to have to walk into a room, sit or lie down and talk about oneself for an hour. It was so unlike any situation one came across in normal life that he saw no way in which it could succeed, at least with him. When he said such things, he knew that he upset her, and so he would qualify them by commenting on the benefits others claimed to derive from the process and that, therefore, there must be something in it.

When finally she got him to agree to see Dr Aaronson, she felt that she had set their relationship on a certain path to happiness and success. Looking back now at that first delirious hope, she pondered miserably that there was no magic in life after all and very few surprises. He never took to Dr Aaronson, a psychiatrist well known for his humaneness and perspicacity and much sought after. The arrangement they made with him was that each of them would see him alone for an hour's session every week, and for the third session, they could see him together, the theory being that the issues brought up in this way would be taken up by each of them in the lone session. As it turned out, and to her bitter disappointment, he regarded the joint sessions as essentially no more than a battleground in which he was under attack from both herself and Dr Aaronson—often, he believed, acting in collusion against him—and his role there was to defend himself as best he could. He loathed having to go and resented her for making him. Though he had appeared in the beginning to listen to her impassioned arguments in favor of the process, when it came to it, he allowed himself to be persuaded only because she wanted it; left to himself, he would not have touched Dr Aaronson or his like with a bargepole.

Dr Aaronson himself pointed this out to her some months after they had started seeing him, but she retained a dwindling hope that he would be ultimately convinced and all would be well. But as time passed, it became clear that he would never accept the process or Dr Aaronson, whom he was antipathetic to. He would go to his sessions, late and bad-tempered as a protest against going at all and would spend what was left of the hour's session engaging in an intellectual contest with Dr Aaronson over abstruse political and philosophical matters. All her hopes that, during these sessions, he would be sorting himself out, learning to understand himself and the problems that plagued him with monotonous recurrence, were gradually dashed.

But she could not give up. She would praise Dr Aaronson extravagantly, recall how often he had helped her, suggest that he talk over this or that problem over with him. In fact, all she succeeded in doing was to make him irritated and even more resistant to opening himself up. She began to feel personally responsible for the fact that, as Dr Aaronson told her, he had made no relationship with him at all in the two years in which he had been seeing him and would leave without hesitation or regret the moment that she said they need go no longer. When she mentioned this to him, his invariable reply was that Dr Aaronson didn't like him and that he in his turn did not trust Dr Aaronson.

After a while, she started to dread the joint sessions and thought more than once of terminating them. Looking at him sitting uncomfortably in his chair in Dr Aaronson's consulting room, obviously wishing he were a thousand miles away, she would feel a mixture of pity and exasperation. The sessions always took the same form. They would arrive late because he usually managed to be occupied until the last possible moment as if to thwart her and Dr Aaronson by stealing time from their hour with him. If she ever showed her annoyance at this, he would fly into a rage, they would then quarrel and arrive for the session barely speaking to each other. Whereas the idea of the therapy was that they should decide beforehand on a topic they wanted to discuss, in fact this seldom happened because, if she mentioned it—and it would have to be she since he never brought up anything of this nature himself—his face would cloud over and his jaw would set in a rigid line which deterred further discussion. They invariably ended up sitting under Dr Aaronson's watchful eye in silence, he staring at the floor sullenly until, unable to bear it any longer, she would start to speak. In all the joint sessions they attended, he never once started the conversation, never brought up any issue, and seemed prepared to let the whole hour pass by in total silence if necessary rather than speak.

Whenever she challenged him about this, his usual reply was that he had nothing to say, he didn't believe that talking helped in any case but that on the contrary it might actually do harm. Why did he attend the sessions then, if he felt this way? "Because," he would answer defensively, "it is thought by those who know best" that it is 'a good thing.'" Whatever this may have meant to him, she understood him to be telling her that while he had acceded to her wish in coming to the sessions, he was damned if he'd do anything else thereafter. He would bring his body to Dr Aaronson's, as promised, but that was all he was prepared to do; his inner thoughts and feelings he would keep to himself. When she complained of some behaviour on his part, since, by definition, he himself would never raise any issues, the session inevitably assumed the semblance of a court of law, in which he was the accused and she was the prosecutor.

Of course, he was no happier than she was and felt just as alone. He blurred the edge of his misery with whisky and overeating, looked at his bloated face and large fat body every morning in the mirror with deep disgust, but carried on eating and drinking just the same. Somewhere inside himself he knew that she suffered and that he denied her what he had himself been denied all his life, but to respond to her hunger would have been to face his own, and he had taken care of that long ago: with alcohol, hard work, and an iron determination to forget. Far better to obliterate the past, to deny all the unassuaged longing, to erect an impenetrable wall between that and the urgent momentary demands of the day-to-day present and thus have only to react to the matter at hand. She and her needs and reproaches could only tug at the suppressed parts of his life, could only evoke unmentionable things that had strenuously to be fought off. Sometimes the mere expression of her face was enough to set him off into a paroxysm of irritation; it was as if she always found him wanting. He would see her looking critically at him as he stroked his cats; he knew that she longed for him to caress her with as much pleasure, she even said it, but the very fact of her longing somehow impelled him to ignore her and lavish even more love on the cats as she looked on.

It was the same with her unreasonable jealousy. He found it stifling and unflattering and felt little sympathy for her anxieties, which actually made him angry. He had dealt effectively with his own jealousy long ago by the simple expedient of never allowing himself to feel it. As a result, he never permitted himself to doubt or worry but rather assumed that if people stayed with each other, then they generally meant to and it was pointless worrying. He thought she ought to do the same and accept his remaining with her as proof of his fidelity rather than the reverse. Her jealousy had forced him to conceal certain aspects of his life from her and he resented doing this. For example, he found himself having to telephone Mandy behind closed doors because she had developed an idiotic notion that there was something between them. Women friends of his, some of whom admittedly he had had affairs with in the past before he knew her, were strictly forbidden from using any but his own private line, in case she became suspicious. He even had to meet them in secret to avoid a row. In all this, he put the blame squarely on her shoulders and felt himself unfairly put upon.

It was all very well for Aaronson to prate about her insecurity and needs, and to treat him as if he were some sort of blind imbecile, but he really did know how she felt. The trouble was that no one cared about how *he* felt, the fact that she imposed her needs on him and demanded that he perform to please her as if he were a stud animal. Her unceasing watchfulness of him evoked painful reminders of long buried horrors which made him recoil. He found her constant probing and desire to talk things through selfish and insensitive, for after all, it served only her needs. Her attitude left him with little alternative but to withdraw, for how else could he protect himself against her attacks? And the more he drew away from her, the more aggressively she came after him, voracious and demanding. At times, it was oppressive and unbearable and he felt his back was against the wall.

No one ever asked him what he preferred to do. If they had, he would have said: let sleeping dogs lie, let things come together quietly, in their own good time; all this pushing and probing can only crush and destroy. In his experience, talking usually led to confrontation and then to anger, it created discord and clarified nothing. He forced himself to participate in the nonsense at Dr Aaronson's because she wanted him to and for no other reason. In reality, he believed it had done more to distance them from each other than anything else he could think of. And if she and Aaronson wondered why he gave her so little of himself, they should look at the way in which they imposed their views on him, demanding for example that he should "work on his problems," as if he were some recalcitrant child who needed to do his homework.

He held it against her that she showed him no esteem. It seemed to him that she had no interest in his work, found him boring and of little account. Because of this, he told her nothing about himself or his thoughts. When she complained that he was shutting her out, he didn't argue. It was true, but it was she who was to blame. By contrast, he took a great interest in her work, helped her with the reports she had to write, advised her on office politics, and listened to her ideas and plans. He believed he had supported her well in her working life, but could look for no similar support from her. It was a familiar scenario for him. Throughout his life, countless people had milked him for help, and had never given him anything in return. He had perforce learned to keep his thoughts to himself and to share nothing with anyone. And so, he always felt alone. He remembered her early on in their relationship asking him to share more of himself with her. If only she knew how much he longed to end his solitude. He had tried to talk to her about ideas that interested him, but he soon noticed that she was bored and he never spoke of it again.

It often seemed to him that his world had been unduly filled with people who did not love him but wanted to control him. To cope with this, he had evolved an intricate system of avoidance and self-defence. People accused him of being touchy, even paranoid, but he knew he had managed to survive because of it. He now found himself needing to invoke this system in his relationship with her; she forced it upon him because of her constant disapproval and the vehemence with which she imposed her wishes and requirements of him. He knew that she was unhappy and felt deprived, but she really had no one else to blame except herself. In his day-to-day dealings with her, he volunteered no information, avoided arguments and discussions, carried out his duties as quietly as possible so as not to excite her criticisms, and was as self-effacing as his large bulk could permit. He saw her impatience and frustration with him, but permitted no opportunity for discussion, lest it provoke a confrontation.

His patience paid off, because at times she responded by being warm and friendly towards him. But he was careful never to respond too hastily himself, in case all his efforts were wasted. And sure enough, her good moods never lasted long. No sooner would he have begun to relax his guard, then she would start a scene usually upbraiding him for his coldness and rejection, apparently unaware that her recriminations only served to alienate him. She thus left him no choice but to withdraw into himself once more and wait for the storm to pass. He lived in hope that she would one day learn to understand him and thus behave in ways which could attract rather than repel him. When that happened, he believed that their relationship would find success. Meanwhile, he waited patiently for her to change and make them both happy.

Directing My Pen Inward

Suheir Hammad

Introduction

After the shock and pain of September 11, 2001, it was Suheir Hammad's riveting poem, "first writing since," that articulated the feelings of many Arab Americans. Widely circulated, the poem embodied many of the feelings of the Arab American community: fear, shock, shame, and defiance at the injustice suffered by people around the world.

Despite her young age, Hammad's voice has become one of the most well-known in the rapidly emerging genre of Arab American literature. Born in 1973, in a Palestinian refugee camp in Jordan, Hammad moved to the United States with her family when she was five years old. She grew up in Sunset Park, Brooklyn, New York, in a neighborhood of Puerto Rican, Jamaican, Haitian, and African American children, whom she befriended. Her identity was shaped by this multiracial and multiethnic environment.

Her first major work was *Born Palestinian, Born Black* (1996), a collection of poems that quickly gained attention for their urban, hip-hop style of expression. Indeed, Hammad traces her literary influences to, among many other groups, African American writers and musicians, and her work is truly an amalgam of multiethnic American writing. Her second book was a memoir, *Drops of This Story*, (1996), solidified her position as a major Arab-American writer.

Hammad also took her poetry live: she starred in *Russell Simons Presents Def Poetry Jam on Broadway* in New York City. *Def Poetry Jam* originally premiered on the HBO network, and proved that poetry can still excite and move audiences and that it was very much current. In one of her poems, "Mike Check," Hammad describes the experience of stereotyping she endures at American airports. Hammad writes also for *Russell Simons Presents Def Poetry Jam on Broadway*, which won a Tony Award.

As much a social activist as she is a creative writer and poet, Hammad ex-
presses herself eloquently on the subjects of war, injustice, domestic violence,
sexual abuse, racism, and homophobia.

~·~·~·~·~·~·~

My poems mark the seasons of my life. All my writing does. I can look at
an essay and remember when I wrote it, what I was trying to say in it.
Whether I thought I succeeded. Poems, however, don't answer to or come
from deadlines and assignments, but the poet's own intimate landscape,
and so the internal shifting that occurs naturally within us over the years
is closely related to the line breaks and the language in a poem.

I am by birth, choice, circumstance, luck, and destiny a poet. While
this is an essay, written in the summer of 2003, I hope you, sweet reader,
will find some poetry in it. I do not know what the world will be like when
you read this. I turn thirty years old this fall, and for the first time in my
life, I can't even begin to wrap my head around what will happen to all of
us, to our planet, in the years to come. My imagination fails me. I have always loved books for this one reason: I might no longer be of flesh when
you read this (I'm not trying to be morbid, but accurate). I aim to leave you
a record of what it felt like, sitting here, using the English language to
make sense and beauty, while the current administration is using "shock
and awe" tactics to achieve a shady goal in Iraq. Maybe there will be no
Iraq when you read this. The United States of America, as I know it today,
may be a very different creature if you find this page even three years from
the time I write it. Maybe Palestine will be free, and you will wonder aloud
how the international community ever let the tragedy of Palestinian dispossession last so long that some of us felt compelled to dedicate our lives
and our work to this one issue.

Or maybe, I will be you. I will be the sixty-year-old reader who can't
remember what it was like to be a Palestinian American poet half a lifetime
ago. And I will come to these words as you do now, with the expectation
of uncovering something about the writer, but also something about myself. That is what we do, isn't it? Read poems and prose of people we hope
have been able to reflect (not capture) some of the human condition. Something, please God, we can relate to. An explanation. An investigation. And,
please oh please, an evolution.

I am going to take a break here and list the names of writers who have
influenced and continue to inspire me. I do this early on in this so damn
self-aware piece, because it's usually one of the last things we do as writers—recognize the continuums we are a part of. Many of us are so intent
on being seen as individuals in our craft that we deny ourselves the company of those who came before us, as well as that of our peers. But I want
to help set the context of my work for you. I want you to go out and read

these people, not only because I love their work, but also because I believe in their work. This is not a disruption of voice. This is voice. Dynamic and layered. You will not only find poets in this short list, because poetry comes from life, not from itself.

Edward Said, Toni Cade-Bambara, Howard Zinn, Sapphire, Noam Chomsky, Chrystos, Etheridge Knight, Audre Lorde, June Jordan, Mahmoud Darwish, Jayne Cortez, Amiri Baraka, Gloria Anzuldia, Bruce Springsteen (yes, y'all), Toni Morrison, Rakim.

Though Bruce Springsteen is included in my list as a writer, he is not the only musician whose work has helped shape my own. My own readers (you may or may not be one of them) drop their jaws when I list him as an inspiration in public discussions, or as an answer to that ever-original question, "Who inspires you?" I know they think a homegirl from Brooklyn by way of Palestine who was reared on hip-hop listens to The Boss? Yes, I do. I listen to George Michael too, but if I even begin to write about that particular obsession, you will have another essay in your hands. I tell younger poets, do not limit yourselves to one kind of music, one school of prose, even one language from which to cull the musicality, the rhythm of your work.

I am looking forward to being you, dear reader, and looking over this list and wondering how I could have possibly left out Constantine Cavafy, Finney, Sandra Cisneros, and others. I am looking forward to finding new inspiration in the years to come. Artists whose work moves me so forcefully out of whatever space I am in that I don't even recognize my hands at the keyboard as they type out words I never used before. This is one of the joys of what I do, the element of surprise, and the hope for evolution. I am looking forward to exclaiming, "How stupid to think you could list all the people who have spirited your life, Suheir."

John Coltrane. Can't forget John Coltrane.

I sometimes need to take a break from reading. This is because I do not read like "normal" people. I have read so many books, I can reread them all over again, and really not remember anything about the story. But I can remember that it moved me. I can remember where I was when I finished a favorite book. If I was in love or heartbreak. What I was eating, listening to, and wearing (something fabulous, surely). I am certain I ruined my eyesight by the desperate midnight hunger I had as a child and into my teen years of reading after the lights were out. I actually read by the light of the street lamp outside of a tenement window. It sounds downright Depression Era, but it happened in 1980s Sunset Park, Brooklyn. I wasn't allowed out "in the streets" much, my parents were traditionalists and strict. I mean Strict. And so, like many people who decide to write their way out of poverty, oppression, solitude and all the isms, I thought if I could bury myself deep enough in a story, I might come out the other side in a different world.

So, I take these breaks from reading, and that's when I usually buy books. To prepare. Like an animal getting ready for the winter, or a mama bird preparing a nest. Even when I am not reading, my life is centered on researching what to read next.

Am I being elusive about all the "why I write" business? I don't mean to be. Truth is, I don't think you can be a writer if you are not a reader. I mean, how can you expect people to buy your work, cherish it, tell people about it, if you don't know what it is like to feel that way about someone else's work? You think your voice so special? It ain't. You think you the only one thought that particular idea up? You ain't.

As a child, I rewrote the endings of stories and plays in my head. I often remark to journalists that I've always written, because reading inspired me to think of new ways of looking at the same things. I didn't have to write it down as much as think it up. I hope my poems can direct young people in that direction—to challenge or confront my work in order to create their own.

I have written or alluded to the words *hope* and *maybe* often in this piece so far. That's the space I'm in right now. In the face of so much destruction, I hope for creation. I know there are writers who fashion themselves "above" politics. They must be living in the clouds then. I live on earth. I dream in the clouds, yes, but I write in a human language for living human beings. Politics are everywhere. I once heard Nawal El-Saadawi speak at a women's forum and say something to the effect that you get two people alone in a bedroom, and there you have politics. True that.

It's not that I read the papers with my notebook open so I can write "political poetry." But I do read the paper, the Net, magazines. I try to gauge where we are in the world. What we are doing to the world. And I try to address where we are coming from, where we are going. We, like me, you, my family, your family. Humanity.

I want to direct my pen inward. Finding so little comfort in corporate media and commercial art, I want to find within myself the hope necessary to create. I believe all acts of creation are reflections of a desire to make clear, distill, and, yes, that word again, evolve. Within me are the East and West and all points in between. I want to find within these lines an inherent poetics of survival. Of Thriving. Of taking a few words and re-arranging them on a page until they form an emotion. I want to feel. Alive.

Poem

---

ramallah walk

i have never seen the bride
gold heavy and made up

step lightly white
pumps in mud
after november rain

i have never seen the
boy of six correct the falafel
man saying i am not
a boy mouth in pout

i have never seen
the falafel man who is a man
of other things at other
times smile and say you
are right my brother

i have never
seen myself walk this
clear morning the moon
still visible in the sky

i have
never seen the sight
of a nine year old blinded
the bullet aimed at the brown
worlds in his face

i
have
never

a
morning walk
moon still visible
rain in the air
falafel stepping lightly in oil
the bride who is other
women at other times
mud in a pout
brothers smiling gold at a
woman walking heavy
brown worlds in her face

Inspiration

Doing What We Can

Naomi Shihab Nye

Introduction

Born in 1952 in St. Louis, Missouri, Naomi Shihab Nye is one of the most well-known and widely respected Arab American writers today. Her first poem was published when she was only seven years old. Born to a Palestinian father and an American mother, she moved with her family to Jerusalem at the age of fourteen; there, Naomi attended a year of high school and reconnected with her father's culture. The family returned to the United States and settled in San Antonio, Texas, where Naomi continued to write. She earned her B.A. from Trinity University, in San Antonio, in 1974.

She is the author of numerous books of poems, including: *19 Varieties of Gazelle: Poems of the Middle East* (2002), which was a finalist for a National Book Award; *Fuel* (1998); *Words Under the Words* (1995); *Red Suitcase* (1994); and *Hugging the Jukebox* (1982). A talented essayist, her prose is gathered in the collection *Never in a Hurry* (1996). Her young adult novel, *Habibi*, was published in 1996 and received high critical acclaim for its touching portrayal of a young Palestinian American girl who moves to Jerusalem with her parents and falls in love with an Israeli Jewish boy her age.

Celebrated for her powerful images and ability to demonstrate the humanity of misunderstood people, Naomi has received many awards, including four Pushcart Prizes, the Paterson Poetry Prize, and Jane Addams Children's Book Awards. A current Lannan Fellow, a recent Guggenheim Fellow, and a Wittner Bynner Fellow (Library of Congress), Nye has also received awards from the American Academy of Poets and the American Library Association.

She lives in old downtown San Antonio, Texas, with her husband, photographer Michael Nye, and their son.

A twelve-year-old girl in Calgary sends a pencil-written letter saying that my novel *Habibi* is her favorite book she has ever read and she is reading it for a second time.

That in itself would be enough to keep me going for the next season.

But she goes on to tell her favorite *sentence* in the book, what details she likes best about each character, and to volunteer that she asked her Canadian mother to cook Middle Eastern food for her while she was reading the book. Also, incredibly, she "placed a white cloth on her own head" while reading the chapters about Sitti, the Palestinian grandmother, who wore a draped white scarf even while she slept.

The girl's own hobbies all start with "s"—silversmithing, sewing, skating, shopping, snowboarding. Because of my one little book, she "will never be the same. I hope you write back."

Forever, honey bun. We write back forever. Back and back, a stitched seam of invisible letters and messages, over and under the pain and glory of the days.

I am so grateful you took the time to find me.

What I don't say: *I wish I could have done more than tell a story. I wish I could have solved things.* But I was not born to be that big.

How does it start? Human-sized, with a pocket of tiny mysteries. Turning a word over and over in one's head as hours go by. Finding comfort in the company of a word. Even an unhappy word like *bossy* or *frustrated*. Discovering where its edges and roots are. *Advice* contains *vice*. No wonder it causes trouble.

Words are not just for *getting things*.

It begins by guarding a secret inner drawer of random observations, as if someone rode around a beautiful small town at dawn on a bicycle, not wanting to miss anything—the break of streaking pink over mountains, a single penny on the pavement where you pause to gaze east, a sloped orchard, a man walking alone along the railroad tracks as a hidden rooster cheers, even a broken white cardboard cup on the floor of the post office.

As you stop to lift it, pitch it into a bin, feeling a flush of energy from pink sky and stirring motion, you hear a subtle swish of letters into postal boxes, from an unseen hand already at work, organizing the day. It's the gift you get for stooping.

Lined-up boxes. Slots in the brain. Troves of syllables. Mine. Yours. Air's.

"Why do you write about ordinary things?" people ask and ask again.

Well, what do they have in their lives?

I never understand that question.
You can't miss it.
Well, yes you can.

Twigs, blown down from the hundred-year-old tree thanks to the stormy outer edge of a hurricane called Claudette.
Name of a storm. Name of a minute.
Scattered around the grass in a curious calligraphy—were they dead on the tree for a long time?
Collect and pile them against the wooden fence.

Moment between moments, the sweetest moment there is? Loving the *almost*. Leave it blank. But think about it.
We could burn the twigs in a pit, grill an ear of corn, a giant potato. Is anything disconnected from everything else?
I wish for peace in the world, but must find it inside every day no matter what else goes on. Chorus humming inside our lives. Someone else was here, we are not the first. Echoes filed in sky.
If you didn't write, what would you do with the fluent river of thought? It would just pile up inside? A dam, a tank? Writing helped thinking and knowing to flow. A mind and body rolled through time. Confusion, isolation? Resolved.
Even on a clumsy day, a little writing nearly always shed more light on things.

"No one ever comes up to me in the hall at school and asks me to tell them about my grandpa," said the blonde high school senior. "Even my family doesn't talk about him, it makes them sad. So I write how he comforted me." She looked down. Tears striped her round cheeks. "I write what he told me to remember. Silly stories. Things no one else remembers. Feels like we're still talking when I do that."

Listening to words inside a certain kind of attentive, gathering silence felt crucial.
Silence that required nothing in return but a slight pause and honor. Before and after they were spoken, words floated in spaces around people.
"To become a poet," all one had to do was read poetry with appetite and care, prickles of connection startled awake. Then one could begin the modest habit of writing things down. A natural progression. I would not feel comfortable "calling myself a poet" till I was in my twenties though. It seemed presumptuous, setting oneself off, while words belonged to everybody.
But not in that way.

Some people did not feel fed by words, words were not their true companions. What was it? Instinct? Why one person became a painter and another kicked a ball? Others could wander with a single word hovering inside for days—*unobtrusive*—and feel as rich as a pirate with a stash of gold.

From the start, language on the page felt better to me arranged vertically. Each word deserved its air. Phrases of a poem magnetized the eye. Space helped each noun and verb to stretch, float, and breathe.

Growing up, trying to pay better attention was any day's goal. Favorite words became *stare, ponder, putter, mull*. Maybe these are the words we grow into after all the drama and desire of youth.

Paragraphs with their compact composure appealed to me, beginning in first grade. I was always waiting for a teacher to invite us to write them again, but none ever did.

So I wrote them for myself.

Love for poems and paragraphs grew into affection for short essays, stories, novels, but always I returned to the poem for sustenance.

Poking around with words. Linking them. Feeling led by them, as they descended, unfurled. Hard to explain. Utterly elemental.

Wandering the cool interior of the St. Louis Art Museum with our mother on Sunday afternoons, we paused long before paintings and sculptures as she described lessons of the artists she'd studied with in school—Philip Guston, Maz Beckmann—what would they say about a given idea or technique? I liked her voice when she spoke in this way. She was descriptive, not directive. It seemed there might be nothing better than a parent speaking about something deeply loved.

We learned *how to look into a painting, not just at it*, a distinct lesson I would attempt to translate into my way of being with words.

The lilt of my Palestinian father's tales blessed every bedside. His gracious old country accent from his first world in the mysterious city of Jerusalem, the funny quotes and sceneries of his tales, donkey, apricots, and wisdoms, cobbled, curling back alleyways in the Old City where he had grown up. He never dwelled too long on troubled politics, since the inequities and losses hurt too much for one in exile. But he created, through language, a place of playful characters and ancient, spicy traditions.

Fixated as I was on my parents (I have written elsewhere about how I never moved out when I went to college, so they finally had to move out and leave me), I also liked listening to people whose names I did not know. Speaking to one another out in public places, catching the far-off calls of kids in the evening, the preciousness of distance and involvement back to back, voices of neighbors sparking the whole air round and about. Somehow, in modern times, the endless one-sided public jabber of cell phone users does not have the same preciousness.

I liked being near enough our small square white house with the open screens in the summer evenings after supper as our mother played the piano and sang. Her voice drifted out on a wave.

And why did a conscious semiprivate relationship with words matter to much?

Regular conversations rarely felt as good.

Daily conversations and arguments too often cluttered space instead of enlivening it. Tangled talk left people in conflict, grated on nerves. Living in a family (particularly a bicultural family, but maybe any family) made us all experts on plenty of *other* word experiences that sometimes ended with muttering, crying, sighing, stalking off, slamming a door. Talk, talk, talk.

Because I was alive in a world where words didn't always work so well between people, I needed to have a one-on-one relationship with words themselves.

The sounds after the sounds, echoes and reverberations. Twilight. Everything sweet and swiftly passing.

My advice (there's that dangerous word) to anyone who asks for it has remained the same for years: read, read, then read some more. Find a way to engage in regular daily writing. It doesn't have to be a huge amount of devoted time (many students write great poems in seven minutes), but a regularity with writing really helps. Consider it parallel to physical fitness. Staying limber, keeping in shape, is not a now-and-then proposition. Writing in small blocks of time keeps us flexible, responsive, in tone and tune with muscular, vivid, energetic words.

Then, find some way to share your work. Become involved in local writing circles, attend readings by writers, familiarize yourself with how much is going on wherever you are. If nothing is going on, start it.

Most writers publish in all sorts of humble places before they publish books. But don't let "rejections" trouble you—they are inevitable, part of the process. Look at your work with a fresh eye when it comes wringing home. Is there any way you could make it better? Toughen up.

How do we keep our courage and patience alive?

Read, read, and then read some more.

A woman recently said to me, "I just wrote a terrific children's book. Too bad no one is publishing children's books these days."

Pacifist that I am, I almost bonked her on the head with my purse.

"Do your homework!" I said. "Wonderful children's books are published all the time, everywhere!"

The reading/writing life forever feels like it is just opening up inside of us, starting freshly.

This is the gift we are given, to see again and again.

Personal Essay

Seatmates

What are the odds? Both my seatmates, flying north and flying south in June 2003, are American soldiers just returned from the war in Iraq.

On the first leg, it's a strong, young woman, buff with radiant hormones, pink-skinned, a trim blonde stand-up haircut, and a bandaged ankle. She's wearing a bright orange "Tommy" T-shirt and is sucking loudly from a tube that stretches under her arm and connects to a camouflaged "camelback" water pouch doubling as a back pillow. I have never before seen such a contraption, so I stare at it. She leans against her own water in her seat, like a portable mini-waterbed.

She tells me she's on her way home from Iraq after a few weeks at a Texas army base for "debriefing" and "leg therapy." No, her wound was not quite in the line of duty—she tripped over a tent stake in the dark. Her unit had commandeered an illicit mini-refrigerator from somewhere so they could keep a stash of cold drinks at all times. Rest assured, there has never been anyone happier to be uninjured. She wishes she had a better story though.

"You have no idea what those sandstorms were like," she says.

Hmmm, maybe I do.

"But how was it for you psychologically?" I ask. "The whole situation of being over there?"

"I can't talk about that," she snaps. She sucks hard.

I return to my book.

But she proceeds to talk nonstop, in a monologue featuring her mates, their high-tech gear, their close camaraderie, what extra provisions and supplies they were able to sneak into their domain, a tiny bit about packing and unpacking problems, the hideous weather, and how they are all missing one another terribly now. She was one of only two women in her unit. She feels guilty to have left them over there, but a wound is a wound, no matter how you get it.

One might think she'd just returned from jolly summer camp. Mates, and schedules, treats and daily recreations. Not a word about pain, blood, bombs, babies mauled in dust, houses of the innocent fallen in around families, and the searing anguish of loss for survivors—how many thousands are dead by now? But all for a good reason, of course. Not a crumble of doubt, not a scrap of an undertone. Think of the pain those people went through with Saddam.

Her ankle is sort of fractured, not totally, but a little bit. Her commander was very mean to her after she was wounded, as if she had tried to get wounded on purpose. He made her finish her shift before she could go see a doctor. She is not missing *him*, that's for sure.

"But did you have any good experiences with the Iraqi people? On the side? Did you make friends with any local citizens?"

She looks at me sharply, as if I just asked her to strip in seat 12B or describe a secret maneuver.

"I told you, I CAN'T TALK ABOUT THAT!"

Then she takes out her deck of "most-wanted" Iraqis playing cards and begins shuffling them in her lap, snapping them back and forth, rearranging the deck.

It is the first time I have seen these cards firsthand. I close my eyes. When they were first reproduced in the newspapers, some of us wondered if the war-is-a-game metaphor had no shame at all. If my seatmate hopes I will admire her cards, she is disappointed.

I pretend to sleep, but the snapping and sucking goes on, the self-absorbed yakkity yak, which old chum she hasn't called yet, what she might do next week.

In my purse under the seat rests a little yellow pair of earplugs that begin to shine in my tactile memory like buried jewels.

I am so glad when our plane lands and she limps off. Flying on to Canada with no one in her seat, I feel even more relieved when the pilot mentions we have just crossed the border.

Thank you. I needed the border.

In Toronto, an American poet friend and I go to dinner. As our salads arrive, he sighs and says simply, "Isn't it nice to be in a country about which one feels no shame?"

I spend a string of beautiful, hot days in Canada. All the people who didn't come to the giant library conference because of their fear of SARS are weenie-dogs. Toronto has 4.5 million people, and very few of them are sick.

On the way back to the airport, my Russian taxi driver turns around in his seat and says, "I have one question: do Americans hate us Canadians now for not being involved in Iraq? I'm worried about that."

Flying home, I change in Detroit and board an odd airbus with a jumbled seating chart—the computer has managed to separate patients from their own small children. The flight attendants ask travelers to move, but many refuse to cooperate. We haven't even taken off yet—how quickly can someone grow attached to a seat?

I switch twice and end up with my second soldier, but that's not the first thing I learn about him. An adorable four-year-old daughter is gripping his hand and he's wearing a NETS basketball shirt. He's so tall I check closely to make sure he's not a Net.

"Hey, I should have worn my SPURS shirt."

He grins. "I'm really for the PISTONS. This was the last thing clean in my suitcase. My cousin gave it to me. I like the SPURS too."

His little girl in the middle seat examines my ring, my watch, my bracelet, my braid. She grins shyly. I examine her purple-haired doll, her barrette, her braid. Then we all settle into eating granola bars.

I'm reading a drove of manuscripts for a poetry contest, one of those activities terrific for the imprisoned.

My seatmate leans over his daughter and looks at a poem in my lap.

"There's an Arabic word in that poem," he says, pointing.

I look up. It's Arabic, yes, transliterated into English, since the poem is taking place in Yemen. I wonder if this is making him nervous, since we're on a plane. I feel very concerned about the sensitivities of cultural identity now whenever I'm on a plane. One would not just toss it around.

"I know it's Arabic because I just got back from Iraq," he says. "My company was in Jordan too. We're a backup unit. I'm studying Arabic."

Now I look at what he's reading in his lap—the Koran, in English. Interesting. "Is that for your class?"

"No, it's just for me. It's good too. Christians who never read it don't know how good it is."

"How was it for you over there?"

"It was terrible," he says, without a pause. "It was a never-ending nightmare of days and nights and it was awful. My fellow soldiers were not kind to the people they met and I couldn't stand it. So I felt a lot of tension in my own company. Their rude, rough behavior broke my heart— old Arab men driving trucks or bringing us fuel or carrying heavy things for us, old gentle men who never hurt anybody, men no more responsible for Saddam Hussein than a hummingbird would be"—(a hummingbird? I liked this guy)—"there was no reason for American soldiers to act mean or cruel to them, but they did. My soldiers acted mean. These were Arab people who were assisting us, you understand, not fighting against us. And I hated it. I made all these Arab friends on the sly, slipped them cool drinks, had to hide it. I'm finished."

"You're finished?"

"I'm quitting the Army."

"You're quitting?"

"I can't stand it. Whatever I do, I have to feel proud about doing it. I learned that from my grandfather who went to prison for being in the Mafia. I'm Italian, can't you tell? All my childhood, I visited my grandfather in prison. My grandma still hates him for getting involved in all that. And he's been dead ten years. He taught me, always be proud. Be proud of who you associate with and what you do and something like this will never happen to you. He used to cry when our visits ended. So I'm quitting."

He tugs his carry-on satchel out from under the seat in front of us, leans over, zips it open, and pulls out proudly—Arabic bread! Spinach pies! A tub of hummus! "Do you know what all this is?" he asks.

"Of course I do," I say. "I'm half Arab." He raised his eyebrows. "Thanks for being nice to my brethren over there. Did you bring this food all the way from overseas?"

"No, I got it in Detroit. Thousands of Arabs there, you know. I ate this food growing up. Along with Italian food."

"Do you think your ability to feel empathy with Arab people overseas was due to growing up in Detroit?"

"Actually," he says, "I went to an all-black high school. I was one of only four students in a class of one thousand who wasn't black. And you know what? Everyone was nice to me. The whole time. Even though I was the other. No one treated me like an other. They protected me. Even now at reunions, I swear they all hug me the most."

"And you're quitting the Army?"

"I'm quitting. Look at me. I'm through."

"What will you do?"

"Anything! Be a manager in a factory! I'm going to start applying this week. After I eat all this food."

Writing Drop by Drop

Dima Hilal

Introduction

Dima Hilal was born in Beirut, Lebanon, and emigrated to the United States shortly before her seventh birthday. The transition to life in America was not an easy one for a small child and an immigrant, and Hilal initially had difficulty understanding that America was her new, permanent home. "On the other hand," notes Hilal, "children are resilient and it's amazing how quickly I picked up the California lingo and ran amuck with friends. It is true however that insecurities often follow a child with an accent and a grandmother who wears a scarf and strange food in her lunch." Her sense of isolation and awkwardness in her new culture is one of the reasons she became fascinated with books and read voraciously as a young girl.

She obtained her undergraduate degree in English with a focus on writing and poetry at the University of California–Berkeley, where she worked closely with and was influenced by the African American poet June Jordan. She also counts among her influences the work of Li Young Li, Martin Espada, Ruth Forman, and Sandra Cisneros, as well as the personal guidance of San Francisco poet Ishmael Reed and Washington, D.C.–area poet E. Ethelbert Miller.

One of the youngest of a new generation of Arab American poets, Hilal has published her poetry widely. Her work has appeared in various literary journals and anthologies, including the *San Francisco Chronicle, Mizna,* and *The Poetry of Arab Women: A Contemporary Anthology.* She has given readings at the Beyond Baroque Cultural Center, the World Stage, the Levantine Cultural Center, the Autry Museum, the Los Angeles County Museum of Art, and the Associated Writing Programs Annual Conference. In 2002, she performed her work at the International Reading Series held at the Alexandria Library in Egypt. She has taught poetry workshops and lectures annually at the University of California—Berkeley on issues of identity, culture, and community in contemporary Arab poetry. She is a member of Tebot Bachs Five Penny Poets, an Orange County nonprofit public benefit corporation dedicated to the support and promotion of strong community, literacy, and personal growth through the art of poetry.

Hilal currently resides in Dana Point, California, where she is working on her first collection of poetry.

～✕～✕～✕～

1983. That year I drew the Lebanese flag on the chalkboard. Wrote my name in Arabic, right to left, in thick loops of white chalk. Earlier that fall, my family had made its way across the Atlantic over the expanse of these United States to the Pacific Coast. I was six years old and the plane that swallowed us seemed massive. I remember running up and down its wide aisles, humming Disney tunes and picturing sunny, magical California. Little did I know then that our ten-day vacation would stretch into weeks, months, and finally years. Even my parents did not realize that they would be uprooting their family, replanting us in a foreign environment in the hopes that we would grow unencumbered by shrapnel and shells. Deep down they may have known that this was a possibility, but to have acknowledged it while packing two suitcases and boarding a flight to Los Angeles would have felt like a betrayal to the country, the brothers and sisters they left behind, to the shirts and pants still hanging in the closet, the food in the pantry. All patiently awaiting our return. If they had acknowledged this nagging suspicion, I am certain that they would have been unable to leave.

In California, my sister and I enrolled in the elementary school across the street from my aunt and uncle's house, where we were staying. I remember walking down a long hallway, my stomach in knots. I looked at the teacher in front of a seemingly endless classroom filled with kids all staring at me, my mouth dry, eyes wide and moist. But my bewilderment slowly turned to encouragement as kids, truly curious about this child from Lebanon, approached me. *Where is that? What do they eat there? Say my name in Arabic!* It wasn't until my second, third, and fourth day at school that curiosity faded into fear. And it occurs to me now that these children were fed that fear at home along with their dinners. *Do you have a bomb? Do you sleep in a tent? Why aren't you all covered up like women in your country?* I nursed these wounds; and eventually these experiences would find their way into poems, they would foster me into a writer.

The following year my grandmother traversed the earth in a similar trajectory to reach us. Teta, our own Scheherezade, a weaver of tales both real and imagined, moved in with my family. A simple visit to the corner store would emit a sigh and a nudge from her. Her keen eye would judge the nervous shuffle of a fellow shopper, the bundle of flowers clumsily grasped in his left hand. "See him?" she'd nod in his direction, whispering on the off chance that he may both overhear and understand Arabic, "He and his wife are in a terrible fight." Or, "He's buying those for his girl-friend who's trying to leave him." Her stories were always colorful and on many occasions, my sister and I would sit on the carpet next to her, en-thralled. Leaning in, we'd implore her to tell us about the time she started a fight on a cruise ship. *Remember, Teta, when everyone's shoes were tossed overboard into the sea?* She would laugh, her eyes squeezing shut and her body shaking with the power of the memory. She would gasp, her words barely finding their way through her mirth, "Thirty of us had to buy slip-pers in the next port!" And like a griot, she would gift us with pieces of our family history that would have otherwise slipped through time's unfor-giving cracks.

I augmented her stories with ones I checked out from the local library, my skinny arms laden with twelve to fifteen books at a time. I read vora-ciously, my imagination stoked by the flames of various authors' words. I read in the backseat of the car, drowning out my family's passionate con-versations. These hours of oblivion would leave me clueless to everyday happenings in the Hilal household: my uncle's birthday party, my sister's day at school, my dad's upcoming business trip. News of these events al-ways took me by surprise, forcing me to bleat indignantly on a number of occasions the now infamous line, "Nobody ever tells me anything!" I read while eating my cereal at the kitchen table (if not a book in hand, then every word on the back of the cereal box). While showering, I read the back of the shampoo bottle. I even read while brushing my teeth, a grace-less act that left water dripping on pages awkwardly weighed down by a tube of toothpaste. I must admit that to this day I still may be caught brushing my teeth at the sink while poring over *Smilla's Sense of Snow* or other books so evocative they manage to hijack me from my daily life.

In my childhood, books served as an escape from my gangly immi-grant awkwardness and newfound shyness. This insecurity was only heightened by my accent and unpopular fashion sense (You mean orange and purple don't match! Jeans at Kids Mart aren't as popular as Guess?). But when my nose was buried in the pages of a book, all of this self-criti-cism faded away. I read enough books to find my way to Berkeley, where this bookworm became a full-fledged English major butterfly. I thrived in the Bay Area, both academically and in its shocking differentiation from my years in über-Republican, ultra-yuppie Orange County. The Bay Area, I found out, was filled with unique characters. I stared in wonder at Pink Man, a gentleman sporting a skin-tight pink leotard that spanned from the top of his head down to his ankles. His costume was complemented by sil-ver wings, which he would flap enthusiastically as he zipped in and out of restaurants and between students on campus, his legs churning madly to keep his unicycle balanced and upright.

In the spring of 1996 my dearest friend, my closest companion, my grandmother, passed away after heart bypass surgery. This devastating and truly maddening experience was followed that summer by reports of an Israeli plane flying over Qana, bombing a UN refugee camp in its wake. I read reports, my blood chilling at tales of blood-soaked shoes, sobbing mothers and heart broken UN workers who stared eyes glazed in shock, at photographers. Having left Beirut in the height of the civil war and immediately after the Israeli invasion that ravished the city, my universe felt like it was imploding. I read every story and watched every television segment until, in the blink of an eye, the headlines disappeared, not even an outline of the story remaining behind.

That summer I went home to live with my family and work full time. I picked up an article written for *The Progressive* by June Jordan, called "Eyewitness in Lebanon." Her words eloquent, haunting, described the crisis back home. I devoured every word, held rapt by this woman's courage, by her humanity, and most of all by the power of her witnessing. I cut out the article, folded it in half and saved it—perhaps recognizing it even then as a lifeline that I could cling to in the face of this erasing, this invisibility. At the bottom of the article, in the fine print of bylines, her name and title stood: Professor June Jordan, U.C. Berkeley.

One autumn day, the sun drenched the streets of Telegraph Avenue in a stunning way only possible in the Bay Area. I sat at Wall Berlin, a grimy café where I all but made the sign of the cross before pushing open the door to the graffiti-scrawled bathroom. That café is where writers went, clad in black, drinking bottomless cups of espresso and chain-smoking over a heated chess game. This is where hair fell dramatically over mascara-lined eyes as they squinted at journal pages covered with furious scrawling. This is where I found myself that September day.

I ran into a friend from one of the poetry workshops I was taking in the English Department and we sat outside soaking up the rare rays. With winter fast approaching, the sun had begun to slink behind thick clouds with increasing frequency. Out of nowhere, we began talking about people we were dying to eventually meet. I leaned forward, strummed my fingers on the table anxiously, and confided, "Do you know who I *really* want to meet? Professor June Jordan."

She looked at me quizzically. "June?" she responded. "Really? She's like my mom."

The next day I trailed her to Poetry for the People, a class held in the bowels of Barrows Hall. I sat in the corner of the room trying to take up as little space as possible. Twelve students surrounded a conference-style table and sat shuffling papers.

June entered the room, sunglasses on. Although much smaller than I had pictured her, she was still immensely imposing. She slid her backpack off her shoulder and set her books and notepad on the desk. She sat down, slowly removed her sunglasses and folded them neatly in front of her. For the next hour and a half, she skimmed through heavily marked passages of a green leather-bound Quran, exploring Islam and its followers with unmatched intensity and challenging her students to think outside of their cultural bounds. The class read Haas Mroue's poetry out loud, the first words of this Lebanese American poet I had ever heard, covering me with goose bumps and making me blink back sudden tears.

Elated beyond words, I approached the professor at the end of the class as she jotted new thoughts down in her notepad. My friend gave me a nudge and gently murmured, "June, this is a friend of mine from my poetry workshop." June said something like, "Uhn." She didn't look up.

"I am so amazed and moved by this class," I gushed. "As a Lebanese and a Muslim I just want to thank you for this, for—"

In the midst of my raving and my genuine gratitude, June lifted her head and stared straight into my eyes. She grabbed my left arm unexpectedly, and with more than a little force, and asked, "Do you want to be in this class?"

I stammered, "Uh, yeah . . . I mean, yes! I would be honored."

And I was.

Our first poetry assignment left me terrified and facing serious issues of inadequacy. For the next week, I procrastinated, which generally involved a great deal of television watching, dishwashing, among other suddenly urgent tasks. When I finally sat down to compose, the blank page was beyond daunting and the verse that spewed from my pen was painful to both reader and poet alike. I vaguely recall scrawling four letter words in a repetitious Tourette's-syndrome-style series across the page. My avoidance techniques eventually paid off, the Gulf War filling my television screen and incensing me beyond belief, the lopsided reporting sending me into fits of rage. In one of these spells, I managed to write "Bedouin Eyes," an emotionally charged poem that aimed to dispel the prevalent view of the Arab as the enemy, a faceless, nameless terrorist. I wrote in a fury, trying madly to convey to the world that those video-game blips on the screen were really resounding blasts, shattered windows, and shaking children.

The next day I brought the poem to class. I shyly read it and after a productive workshop, June motioned me over. She smiled and said, "I'm doing a commentary called 'Flashpoints' on Pacifica radio. Would you allow me to read this poem?"

Before I could even utter *of course*, or *duh* or *hell ya*, June had paused, reflected, and continued, "Actually, why don't *you* come read it yourself?"

Over the next few years I would learn that I would follow June anywhere and, more often than not, I would arrive in a place well outside my comfort zone, somewhere both bewildering and magical: teaching a poetry workshop to a transvestite named Brenda, protesting in front of the CNN building, on a blind date arranged by a sheepish June. No matter what the occasion, I would soar in her company. We all did, her students. By sitting next to me in the studio, my first ever public reading, with the surround sound of monstrous headphones and an oversized microphone at my lips, June put her faith in me and my words. She introduced me with a poignant segment on Middle East events. I can still hear the pride and strength in her voice: "And I give you nineteen-year-old Arab American poet . . . offering you her words, her heart, and her hurt." I read nervously, mechanically and it still sounded amazing nestled between her intro, and conclusion. I am convinced that I easily could have recited the "Pledge of Allegiance" or my car manual and, with her by my side, it would have come across as music.

I continued to write, but with a new consciousness. I was no longer writing to get thoughts out of my head and onto paper, a private expression in which poetry served as my form of journal writing. Now I had discovered that my words could have an audience. My poetry could impact and inform another human being in a real, meaningful way. How exhilarating. How utterly terrifying. Connecting with others had an element of nakedness for which I was entirely unprepared. Speaking in front of people was one thing; reading my own deeply personal and emotionally charged work was quite another, thank you very much. After enduring the exhibitionism that comes from reading in front of large audiences, I came to an uneasy truce: I could read in front of hundreds of people, provided that my poems were true and meaningful. And so I did just that, I wrote from the heart about my family, the old country, Palestine, issues that flowed through my veins.

Poems

you got some nerve

we stand face to face
but you do not see me
through your blindfold
woven with ideals
I give my voice to Palestinians
hold up pictures of them dying
but you shut your eyes

absolve your country
even when I tell you stories
of tanks and guns and shelling
day after day
still I hear your excuses
we must protect our citizens
it makes me want to yell
you got some nerve
I listen to you rationalize
half apologize
it's a matter of defense
and I want to cry
no!
take you by the hand
show you mine feels like yours
no!
and pull you
with my urgency into the sky
no!
and pull you
to olive trees and dry earth
point to children
and say, I know you have eyes
can't you see
they cannot grow here
in a refugee camp
they will never feel strong
looking over their shoulders

you got some nerve
to speak of saving lives
my people give birth to death
every day
to speak of land
we sift through ashes
you got some nerve to even imagine
we do not have a god to pray to
I want to grab both your shoulders,
ask, just what do you think
we need refuge from anyway?
and I crouch to the ground
put my lips to dust

curl my head back to the sky
and howl
and dare you,
I dare you to say
you still don't believe me

Mediterranean Breeze
for June

We walked along the Corniche
watching the sea change colors
as the sun set,
a fisherman cast his line
one last time

We played cards
inside building corridors
your laughter louder than
the throb of my veins,
the thunder of shells falling outside

You taught me
to let the Mediterranean breeze
slip between my shoulder blades,
across the round of my belly to my toe
lifting up my every step

You told me to speak my mind
louder than the sound
of falling shells
as loud as your laugh
skimming rooftops
and climbing into morning sky

america

we cross from Andalusia to these Pacific shores
we carry memories in a single suitcase
abandon brothers, skyscrapers and tight alleyways
villages framed with grape leaves and fig trees
the land of Jesus and Abraham

we flee fighter jets and darkening skies
escape shrapnel scenes,
for the American dream
we brush off dust from the old country
unearth the clay from beneath our nails

we fade into the fabric of these united states
pay our taxes, pledge our allegiance
lose ourselves in its thick folds
success finds us and we find success
intoxicating

until a plane carves a path through steel and glass
smoke billowing from two wounded skyscrapers,
the aftermath all too familiar
just the epicenter shifting
we know the endless sorrow
of life snatched without warning or reason,
we seek solace in our neighbors
see our own blanched faces
reflected back at us

until the sudden sidelong glance,
the step back
wait, isn't that where you're from?
let's bomb them back to the stone age
those arabs
never should have let them into our country
those arabs
never should have let them in
we'll show them
those arabs
we'll teach those turban-wearing, towel-headed,
dirty, motherfucking, camel loving, terrorists
a lesson they'll never forget
fractured skull, baseball bat,
crushed bones, clenched fists
battered bodies, a switchblade, crow bar
gun shot blast

it's us versus them
are you with us
are you with us

are you with us
or against us?

born by the Mediterranean,
our mothers bathe us in orange blossom water
olive trees and cedars strain to give us shade

we cross from Andalusia to these Pacific shores
we flee fighter jets and darkening skies
escape shrapnel scenes,
for the American dream
for the American dream
the American dream

Memory

The Relentlessness of Memory

Elmaz Abinader

Introduction

Born in 1954 in western Pennsylvania, Elmaz Abinader first began writing in 1971. Her first book was a memoir of her family, entitled *The Children of the Roojme, A Family's Journey from Lebanon* (1991), a chronicle of immigration that depicted the struggle of people living in the last days of the Ottoman Empire and highlighted the pain of adopting a new homeland. The memoir grew out of a postdoctoral fellowship in the humanities, during which she studied with Toni Morrison.

While her first major publication was a memoir, Abinader's work spans several genres. In 1999, she published *In the Country of My Dreams*, a collection of her poetry that went on to win the PEN Oakland Award in 2000. Her verse portrays the struggle of Arab-Americans living between cultures. She also writes and performs plays, including the most recent, *Under the Ramadan Moon*, a two-act play set in Cairo, in which she explores the theme of acceptance into the Arab culture. An accomplished essayist and critic, Abinader has contributed to numerous anthologies and journals. She is also cofounder and that faculty and board president of the Voices of Our Nations Arts Foundation, which organizes writing workshops for writers of color.

Abinader lives in Oakland, California, and teaches at Mills College.

Memory knits me, puts me together with each stitch, crossing over my days and under my nights. Each stroke is simple—a whisper, a name, an action. The needles click a Morse code of history, a clave beat of journey; the cadences that came before me; the drumming that will move me on. I hear the throb of memory pulse through my body like a *dabke* (line dance), emanating out of my legs with a kick, being received with a stomp—connected to the earth and near to flight.

Memory wraps me. A blanket in the making. What is familiar, simple to recall, and gets me through my day, comforts me. I know where I come from: what cultures, what country, what family; whom I come from: what peoples, what parents, what DNA; and I recognize what memory has left on me. The certainty of origin warms me against the unsteadiness of a world that does not know me.

Memory lives in my body. My face remembers—my eyes sink deeply in small darkened sockets like Sitti Elmaz's, chestnut brown specked with gold. My cheeks avalanche toward my jaw—my mother's jowls that softened toward her chin on her otherwise wrinkle-free face. Her nose hooks on me, long and thin over a slender mouth. My hips remember oil jars balanced on the head, although I have never carried them, my legs remember rocky hillsides, hard to climb to lead the cattle into shelter for the night; my arms remember bundles of mesquite carried to the charcoal pits. Centuries of women's lives fill me. My body holds memories in its form and feeling, in sense and sympathy.

Memories are inherited and acquired. The moment of experience transforms immediately from event to memory. The evolution of that instant never ends. Each time a story is told, something changes. The difference may be as subtle as an intonation or as pronounced as time or place. Memory is not to be trusted for it is unstable and is affected by perspective, character and consequence.

I grew up a listener. All the children in our family understood that we had two roles, obeying and paying attention. To impose the latter was hardly necessary because we were an eager audience to the great storytellers in our family: our father and aunt and great-uncle. The large family dinners were the primary venues for these performances. I anticipated the moment long before it began, even while the dinner was in the making. As I beheaded parsley for tabouleh or set the dining room table, I considered which of my father's stories I hoped he would tell. Many were favorites: one in which the donkey, carrying the vegetables, is attacked by insects and the animal ends up rolling down the hillside, squashing everything in its packs. Or the other in which my mother and father decide to marry: my mother's eyes shone when my father claims he was a reluctant groom, dragged to the altar with a large noose around his neck.

Throughout dinner, I watched the food circle the table, the adults served themselves one dish after another. I wiggled my leg, bounced in my seat. Afterward, my part in the clearing and cleaning was performed with speed and efficiency. The stage would be the living room, the props would be cups of Arabic coffee for the adults and soda pop for the children. *Baklava* and cookies sat on porcelain saucers. I listened intently for the moment the Arabic conversation gradually turned into a story told in English.

I never knew if there was some consideration at that moment for us children who didn't understand Arabic, or if my father meant to tell the stories in English, but he did. By the time I was seven, I had heard them all. The joy of listening became learning that this life, in this foreign land where bread was cooked in public ovens and figs were stirred in giant pots to make a sweet treat, was, in fact, my history. The intrigue of the familiar stories was what new detail would be added or what description omitted. The tales often became interactive, with my mother or my uncle adding details or refuting information. These stories became as organic as counting— something that one doesn't have to remember each time, but just performs.

I also own memories I did not hear through stories, which were not, in fact, experienced. Instead they were inherited, were stored someplace in my body. When I wrote the memoir, *The Children of the Roojme: A Family's Journey from Lebanon*, I accessed diaries and letters that existed in the family archives; I interviewed elders, researched histories, visited the family village in Lebanon. The final product was a book of three generations of AbiNaders who preceded me: their lives in Lebanon and their subsequent journey to the United States.

In the scenes of the family, in intimate moments, I had to create dialogue and behavior that felt credible. Using what I saw in my parents and my aunt, remembering my grandmothers and great-uncle, I imagined how they would interact early in the twentieth century. The book drove me through the characterizations and, sometimes, I just poured forth, being led by instinct and hunger.

My mother's response to reading the book was, "How did you know?" For example, I described her internal conflict on the morning after her wedding when she refused to hang the wedding sheet off the balcony of her mother's home in the village. I created the moment in her bed, sweaty and grieving, after she gave birth prematurely to her first child who didn't live.

"How did you know?" She was anxious. I didn't know what to tell her. As far as I was concerned, I didn't know; I remembered.

Memory is housed in the body, not the mind, I believe, despite the theories about brain hemispheres. How it gets there does not concern me. It comes by faith and constancy. Paying attention to what one holds, what constructs us, and what we have inherited are vital, especially for one who wants to access memory.

The catalogue of memory is impossible to control. And each item does not exist in and of itself; memory is sloppy and inconsiderate of order. Our stream of consciousness is both random and associative, so while cooking and remembering a recipe my mother taught me, a song my Sitti Marwa sang may enter the scene.

I cannot control memory; I can only heed it and see how it informs me. I pull from it, one thread at a time.

I remember prayer: the cadence, the luxurious language, the intent, the praise, and the extension of belief. I also remember the subordination of the self, the sense of gratitude for life and its gifts, the confidence that solitude and isolation are not our fate. I remember prayer as community— a family who knelt together at night, reciting the rosary together. We rolled the incantations over our tongues in harmony, each voice mumbling the response. My shoulders ached and my knees pressed into the unforgiving tile floor.

I remember singing: my mother's tinny voice imitating Judy Garland and the carefree tunes of the Big Band era; her grabbing one of us children to do a quick jitterbug in the kitchen between cooking and laundry. Choir songs, Girl Scout rounds, glee club performances, pop music and Motown hits mix with the tunes of a carousel, the church organ, my first guitar, piano lessons, and my father singing three lines in Portuguese that he remembered from his youth in Brazil.

I remember dancing: *dabke* and belly dancing when the dining room table was moved aside. Long lines of relatives stringing throughout the house, yelling and stomping as if they were not thousands of miles away from a home where they preferred to be. Someone waving a handkerchief, someone shaking fiercely. The house itself sprung up and down with the relentlessness of the bodies whirling out of memory.

I remember cooking: cumin, parsley, mint, thyme, cinnamon, cardamom, anise, garlic, lemon, and onion. These smells roll between my forefinger and thumb, rise from my skin, fill my hair. The women share a chrome and red table with vine leaves and bulgur wheat, eggplant, and chickpeas. Chopping, rolling, folding, mixing, grinding, squeezing, tasting, mashing, and serving. I am seasoned with it.

Along with the conscious and unconscious stamping of physical and mental memory is the inherited history that comes from story, song, example, philosophy, culture, society, family, behavior, action, roles, rules, lore, and mythology, as well as the magical infusion of unknown and unnamed memories. They accompany me into a stichery of the story of a life, others' or mine, as I try to give stability to an ever-changing past.

Creating a scene of my mother as a young child includes the language of our conversations, the shrug of her mother's shoulder. She is a young child emigrating with her mother from Lebanon. I become the cartographer of her journeys, not because I learned about them, or traveled them myself, but because I remember them. She climbs the stairs from steerage to second class and flirts with passengers willing to feed her. They smile at her chubby face, stroke her light brown curls. At Ellis Island I run with her as she dodges the inspector who will spot her bad eyes and send her home. She pushes her way through the crush of bodies to a corner where she slides against the wooden floor, out of sight, but where she can see her mother at the desk, shrugging her shoulders.

I *use* memory and *serve* memory in order to capture a flash of history lived through very particular characters' lives. Although I imbue my writing with imagery of knowledge and imagination, it becomes semidocumentary because it suggests a specific life in a political and geographic time frame. Through this tiny speck, some awareness may be shared about families living through events that are large flashes across news programs. My characters are not representatives, although their lives are a testimony to the effect of political decisions on one family, village, or character.

We can live with a family whose son is a Palestinian X-ray technician. On his wedding day, chairs are borrowed and placed in a circle in the dirt for the elders to sit on while the couple dances through the crowd. Everyone claps and toasts the couple; someone chimes a glass over and over, commanding them to kiss. Four days later, he is walking to the hospital with some colleagues when an Israeli missile tears through the sky and falls in front of them, exploding like the end of the world. And the chairs are borrowed again, and placed in the dirt, where neighbors mourn these deaths.

My characters are tiny warriors against the massive media machine that does not see them at all; these stories are the small stones thrown in a battle too large to win.

When I write my family stories, I don't imagine myself grappling with political giants or media monsters. I am a storyteller. I access the elements that hold memory and mystery, imagination and imagery to freeze the fluidity that transforms the constellations of our past.

Some people write memoirs to find themselves. I prefer to go to memory to lose myself in the insistence of the past and its secrets. The supply of insight is endless. My readers don't recognize these stories as a mere run of stitches in a large cloth, but see each knot as a capsule of a world they have come to know primarily through sound bites and filmed reports.

For the people about whom I write, this is vital for historical integrity. If a story is never told where one can be in the house of a Lebanese villager, or on the road with a Palestinian student, their reality does not exist for the reader. No portal is available for imagination or empathy to enter. Living life is the only true common element between people, and so I write about the days rather than the years of my characters.

Just as the past redefines itself every day, the nature of memory does not allow my stories to end, leaving me the servant of memory and its master as well. Nevertheless, whether I am writing in play, prose, or poem form, every stitch shared provides a common experience that serves more purposes than I ever intend.

Personal Essay

Our People: Pennsylvania, 1959

People are coming. The mother is gazing at a leg of lamb roasting in the top oven. She drops the door shut then pulls the rice off the stove. Her heels click across the kitchen linoleum as she moves back and forth between counter and stove, table and cupboard. She has placed a full smock apron over her church dress and has taken off her hat with the light blue veil. A line of platters covers the tabletops. Middle daughter surveys the spread; these are her favorite foods: stuffed grape leaves, *humus, baba ghanouj*, stuffed squash, rice pilaf, green beans, *kibbe, tabbouleh* salad, Arabic bread, and yogurt. The top oven holds the leg of lamb her father will soon slice, and in the bottom oven are three pear pies made with the fruit they canned last year.

The kitchen and dining room open onto each other with a little step in between. Everyone seems to be going up and down, over and over, helping with the preparations. All the children have jobs: the older sister is making the cookie tray, placing the anise cookies on the outside, the diamonds of baklava in the middle. She decorates it with red, green, and black gumdrops and licks the sugar off her fingers. The middle daughter is setting the table in what their mother calls "buffet style." She raises up to stack all the dishes at one end of the table—twenty-four in all, her mother counted from memory. For company, the paper napkins are designed like a man's handkerchief which requires a tri-fold—each end to the middle. The middle daughter carefully pulls the edges to the center and starts to crease the sides. Her hands are slow and fumble a bit, causing one edge to go askew. She has to refold them over and over. As her mother passes her with trays of food, she scowls, "Aren't you finished yet?" The middle daughter quivers in response and ends up crossing them unevenly again.

The brothers are setting up tea trays and card tables in the living room and dining room. They go in and out of the house carrying extra chairs. The basement door is open as soda and jars from the pantry are brought up. The grandmother places parsley sprigs on the humus in a pool of olive oil and the mother shapes raw *kibbe* into an oval loaf, pressing the lamb and bulgur and smoothing it along the sides. When she finishes, her mother steps forward, denting the loaf with the side of her hand, making the shape of the cross. Sitti cries a prayer with a long wail at the end.

Voices are crashing in the upper atmosphere, the middle daughter thinks. She knows her mother is yelling about time passing too quickly and the more she complains the more knotted her daughter's fingers become. Her father breaks up chunks of ice for his special punch, offering everyone a taste out of the tin measuring cup. "Enough sugar?" he asks after pouring two streaming cups into the pot. Sitti prays loudly, pushing tissue inside the pocket of her outer sweater. The children say nothing.

The brothers have been allowed to take off their ties, but the daughters are still in their Sunday dresses. The middle daughter feels the edge of her shoe bite into her skin. During church, her foot swelled around the one cross strap of her shoe. It left a ridge in her skin that she will run her finger over later when she is sitting in bed. She wishes she could at least unbuckle them, but mother reminds her: *People are coming. Our people are coming.*

A small chill of excitement runs up the middle daughter's legs. She loves the smothering atmosphere of the crowd that will soon arrive and fill their house. These people, *our* people, are the collection of cousins and aunts and uncles who come from other towns in Pennsylvania: Uniontown, Fairchance, Donora, New Castle. They are not the people who live in town, those who have only been in their house for card parties. They are not the guests who look at the kibbe, the brown little footballs of lamb and cracked wheat filled with nuts and ground meat, and ask, "You eat that?" They are not the people from church or customers who go into her father's store and try on everything and buy nothing. These guests arrive with kisses, crashing the walls with Arabic choruses, grabbing each other in large hugs, faces to each side, one then another, and back again.

The middle daughter finds herself constantly under them and their giant gestures, where the purses of the women slide down to the elbow and nearly hit her in the head. She moves around their legs: the wing tips of her uncle B, the seamed hose of her aunt A, the movie star sandals of her women cousins. The middle daughter swims through their bodies as she tries to see who the latest arrival is. Her aunt Nora with the hump bends toward her and crows a question in Arabic. The middle daughter sways a little before she answers. And her husband, Ray, not an Arab, but a true red-faced American, grabs her by the shoulders and shakes her a little. "You gonna talk now?" he laughs.

The middle daughter is used to Ray and his teasing. The relatives who live close by meet their family once a month at the Maronite church where her mother's uncle is the pastor. It's "Uncle's church" to them, where they talk endlessly outside the door, and then at the church breakfast and later in the rectory. She knows their names, their jokes, the sound of their voices when they sing in the pew behind her.

It's the other cousins the middle daughter watches with greater interest, the ones who come from New Castle and Donora. She never remembers their names; from one visit to the next, she squints up at Mr. Sarkis: Is he Philip? Paul? The wife, Noreen, looks like a quiet movie star; her mother says she's *"black Irish."* The middle daughter keeps watch at the door, hoping some kids are trailing behind the parade of adults, but the house fills with stockings and suits and hats and coats for the children to collect and hang up.

At these special dinners, everything happens in lines. People circle the table neatly behind one another. The conversation is thick as they grab the spears of shish kabob, the stuffed grape leaves, slices of the leg of lamb, the green bean stew, and platter after platter steaming into the clouds of words above them. The middle daughter watches the food pile on the plates. They complete a revolution and the line breaks up as each adult searches for a place to sit and eat. The children wait until the table is free and all the adults are resting from the dance.

The children take the melmac plates, not the china ones. The middle daughter holds hers with both hands. She reaches on tiptoe to get the *laban* (yogurt) spooned onto her plate. Yogurt is served with every meal and the middle daughter puts it on everything, even the tabbouleh salad, mixing it up till it looks like "vomit," the middle brother says. They sit at the children's table, two card tables unfolded and covered in a vinyl cloth. The middle daughter swings her legs as she eats, listening to the adults tell stories, watching them wave forks in the air and stuffing bread covered with humus into their mouths.

The line dance resumes: her aunt gets up and takes the dishes to the kitchen, the men walk out to the yard and look at the garden. The children weave in and out as they travel the route from earlier in the day, picking up the extra chairs, shaking out the tablecloth, moving the table back together. The daughters serve dessert in the living room: pie, coffee and *baklava*, and soda and cigarettes. Sometimes huge happy slices of watermelon, which the middle daughter remembers in Arabic sounds like "buck teeth."

The sisters work hard, following the commands of the adults to bring out the cookies, ask the uncles what kind of Nehi they want, put the chalky mints with the jelly filling into the pink glass candy dish. The middle daughter doesn't mind; it makes her a small part of the line dance.

There is a minute. Who knows how it starts, maybe when the striped dishtowel is hanging to dry, when Mother's apron is back on the hook in the pantry, when the men's collars are open and the women's lipstick is faded, a time when they end up in the living room sitting on the thick couches and the straight-back chairs. The children cross-legged on the rug. The middle daughter drops her skirt over her knees and positions herself between her sisters.

Sometimes only one envelope has arrived, sometimes more. Sometimes an uncle or aunt brings one along. They are sheer and crinkly in their red, white, and blue envelopes with the airplane on them and "par avion" printed in someone's hand. And when the ceremony commences, everyone is silent. The father, the chosen reader, holds the letters far away from his eyes as he follows line after line.

It is this moment that the Arabic becomes music for the middle daughter. It is flute wind circling the room through the red thick curtains, across the pictures on the piano, around the horse-head lamps, weaving through the chandelier, and into the eyes and ears of the listeners. These letters from the *old country*, from home, from the ones left behind, stir their emotions. Some news makes their faces knot, some sentence sends a gasp through the room. Large tears roll down cheeks into monogrammed handkerchiefs and striped dishtowels. Father clears his throat as he works his way through the words, his volume shifts high and low.

The middle daughter has studied all the relatives in the pictures that come with these letters. In the center of each is Sitti Elmaz, her father's mother, after whom she was named. Sitti Elmaz wears black and pulls her hair off her round face. They describe her as five feet by five feet, laughing at her square body. But it houses incredible power according to the people in the room, as she is the family matriarch and rules the village and fifty-odd children, grandchildren, cousins, and neighbors around her. She, the queen, the grand dame. Even the middle daughter's mother speaks of her mother-in-law with admiration. She still bakes her own bread, to this day, the Mother muses. The middle daughter studies the photo, sees an old woman with a line of a mouth—no crown, no cape, or staff. An old round lady, hair under a dark scarf, unsmiling and dressed in black. Sometimes in the middle of the silence, her father says, "I want to see my mother."

The middle daughter cries when they cry even though she doesn't understand any of the words. She is mesmerized, not by the letters, but by the melancholy of the adults when they hear from their families. It is a Greek chorus, a call and a response, a hue and a cry. A letter from father's brother makes Uncle ask questions. The paper is waved away as arguments begin about property or building in the village in Lebanon. Aunt sneers a remark about someone who got married, or didn't. Then it is quiet again and the flute finds its melody once more.

In the mystery of the language, the middle daughter anticipates the turn, the moment after the letters are put down, stuck back into the pocket of the gray jacket father wears. The point where the adults are talking in Arabic about something, their parents, life in the old days, how they miss home. And who knows why, but at some point, their father switches to his thick dense English to tell a story of when he was a little boy. The children scoot forward.

Is it possible that their great-uncle Shebl, turned toward a bull charging the boy's father, and shouted, "Stop!" and the bull halted in his tracks? Can they believe when their father fell off the roof of the house, when everyone thought his life was over at six years old? But someone slaughtered a lamb and brought his skin to wrap the child and warm him back to life? Some stories are repeated so often, Elmaz thinks she can tell them herself. Or they are her life instead of her father's.

Elmaz holds these stories close and tells them to herself over and over. It makes her father glamorous in a way she knows no other kids understand. She tries to picture him on the Amazon with wild animals and raging waters around. He scares her almost all the time with his abrupt speech and shouting. How can she imagine him sitting next to his mother, a sickly child?

In the lull that follows the tales, the happy silence, another transition is heralded by their grandmother. Sitti releases a *zaghrut*: Putting her hand to one side of her mouth, she flicks her tongue in a trill, a high pitch twirl, that starts everyone clapping. The mother rises, and twists her way to the phonograph and drops the needle on an Eddie Kolchak record, her favorite Arabic musician. The drums and oud twist a dancing tune into the room and the house seems to open up, to no longer have doors and halls and curtains and furniture. Everyone joins arms and dances the *dabke*, the final line dance of the day. Sitti claps the rhythm as she sits on the couch swaddled in her sweaters. The American husband, Ray, steps outside for a cigarette. But everyone else is linked at the arm snaking their way through the living room, the hall, and the dining room. The middle daughter reaches her hand to her sisters and lets the dance begin to move her around. When she can feel her feet land on the red and gray marbled linoleum, she joins them as they stomp, kick, and step three crossovers and stomp, kick, and step again.

The *zels* ring in her ears, the small finger cymbals that her cousin has attached to her finger and thumb. The mother comes into the center and wiggles a small belly dance, smiling through her gray shining eyes, waving her arms and tilting her hips. Her face is luminescent and her arms bird wing through the air, around the heads of her guests, up to the sky, out to the side. She grabs at the men to bring them in, and one rises and shakes his belly back and forth and everyone laughs and claps. Someone pulls out the white handkerchief to twirl a surrender to the music, crouching and rising on the end of the line.

Inside the beat of these drums, the wind of the flute, the middle daughter feels Elmaz inside of her as her back shakes loose, her shoes release their grip on her feet and she floats in the wave of stomp, kick, and, three crossovers. The youngest sister moves to the center and dances with the mother. They proclaim in Arabic how cute she is as she rocks from the front leg to the back, up and back. Elmaz keeps kicking and stomping and doesn't stop. She's on a high speed train that is taking her far far away from town, far away from the church down the hill, far far away until the record is over and it's time to bring everyone Arabic coffee.

Along Main Street, outside their house, the cars curve up over the hill and into town, or down toward West Virginia. The homes are quiet, flashing with television or filled with light drenched on board games. Elmaz imagines this from the conversations her classmates have together; she's never been to anyone else's house but her aunt's. From the outside, the houses seem organized, with bushes all the same height, curtains pulled back neatly, lawns without the yellow spots of dandelions that plague their yard. She doesn't imagine that the folks who live in them, like her family, are now standing in the living room singing together as the youngest brother, the one who is best on the piano, plays songs from the 88-popular-tunes book. And how the middle brother can sound like Johnny Mathis when he sings "Chances Are." How their mother, full of music, shakes her finger in the air like Cab Calloway when they sing "Camptown Races."

She doesn't know if they too are drinking coffee in tiny demitasse cups where grounds cake in the bottom. Do they turn the cup over to let the grounds shape into a picture, forming the map of their future? An aunt squints at the patterns in the bottom, turns the cup around and around. All images that form on the ceramic surfaces are prophetic visions. The mountain that represents the difficulties ahead for the drinker. Sometimes she sees a person who, like a chicken, will betray them. Elmaz has looked into these cups with their lumps of coffee here and there and does not feel a gypsy inside of her interpreting lives from the sooty configurations.

What the middle daughter does know as she sits, leaning toward sleep that she is *Elmaz* here with dark hair, and deep brown eyes, and a curvy body. No Elma Ann, the shy girl at school, afraid to speak. And when the adults say, "Good night," or touch her cheek, they distinctly call her *diamond*. "Naim, ya Elmaz." *Sleep, Diamond.* And she will dream this in her restless night. A diamond sea, a flute wind, lines of dancing, and crying and joy. She will chew Elmaz in the conversation of her dreams.

A Life of Stories

Diana Abu-Jaber

Introduction

Diana Abu-Jaber was born in 1960 in Syracuse, New York, although her family did not stay in one place for long. Her Jordanian father and American (Irish-German) mother decided to move the family to Jordan when Abu-Jaber was seven years old, although they only stayed for two years. Ever since, Abu-Jaber has made her home somewhere between the United States and Jordan.

Abu-Jaber credits her father with influencing her to write; specifically, she credits strories he recited to her and her sisters when they children with sparking her imagination. She pursued writing as a college student, graduating with a Ph.D. in Creative Writing from State University of New York—Binghamton in 1986.

Her first novel, *Arabian Jazz* (1993), was the first book by an Arab American writer to garner wide attention by the mainstream media. Set in upstate New York, the novel is a humorous take on the lives and struggles of a first-generation Arab American family. The novel's main character is Jemora (or Jem for short), who must navigate between the ties she feels to her extended, eccentric family and those that draw her more and more into her very American upbringing. Though *Arabian Jazz* won the Oregon Book Award and was a finalist for the National PEN/Hemingway Award, the novel caused much controversy. It received mixed reviews from the Arab American community, some of whom dubbed the comical perspective on its Arab characters as an extended stereotype. Other reviews, however, celebrated the novel for bridging the gap in a general American understanding of Arab culture.

A National Endowment for the Arts Award winner, as well as a winner of a Fulbright Research Award, Abu-Jaber published her second novel, *Crescent*, in

2003. Its protagonist is again a young Arab American woman caught in an identity crisis: Sirine is an Iraqi American and a chef who never thought too deeply about her ethnic heritage until she falls in love with a handsome Iraqi literature professor. *Crescent* received critical acclaim as well, cementing Abu-Jaber's role as a notable American novelist.

Abu-Jaber has published numerous short stories in literary magazines such as *Ploughshares*, the *North American Review*, and *Story*. Her work attempts to narrow gaps of misunderstanding between communities. During the American bombing campaign over Afghanistan, she published a short story about an Afghan family whose father was lost during the evacuation; the story, entitled "For the Time Being," appeared in *Good Housekeeping*, a mainstream women's magazine.

Abu-Jaber currently lives in Florida and is working on her next book, a food memoir, entitled *The Language of Baklava*.

◦~◦~◦~◦~◦

I grew up inside the shape of my father's stories. A Jordanian immigrant, Dad regaled us with tales about himself, his country, and his family that both entertained us and instructed us about the place he'd come from and the way he saw the world. These stories exerted a powerful influence on my imagination, in terms of what I chose to write about, the style of my language, and the form my own stories took. My father taught me, through his example, that one of the best ways to shape reality was through the telling and imagining of stories.

People often ask me about my American mother, and whether she also told stories. Actually, my mother is not a native storyteller in the way my father is, but it may be that she has taught me something even more valuable, which is how to listen to stories. She made a space in our home for my father to invent himself, and her attentiveness and focus showed me that sometimes being quiet can be just as transformative as speaking. She was a reading teacher at the local school and every week she brought me armloads of books—I was especially passionate about mythology, legends, fairy tales, and science fiction. I was in love with magic and the idea of a magical world, full of possibility, in part, perhaps, because my own life experience was a bit magical. I lived between America and Jordan, like the mermaid who was neither fully human nor fish—I knew myself to be a creature of the in-between.

I have two younger sisters and we grew up in little snowbound houses in Syracuse, New York, and then spent some time living among courtyards and trellised jasmine and extended family in Amman, Jordan, before we all moved back to Syracuse again. My father could not make up his mind about which country we should live in. In America, he constantly reminded us that we were good Arab girls; we weren't allowed to go out to parties or school dances. But then he encouraged us to study single-mindedly, to compete as intensely as any boy, and to always make our own way in the world.

My father's brothers are doctors and scholars and politicians. And it was determined that I would receive my undergraduate degree from State University of New York–Oswego because one of my uncles taught there and could keep an eye on me while I lived in a dormitory. When I finally struck out on my own to do my graduate work, I instinctively sought out mentors—the next best thing to uncles, in my mind—going for my M.A. at the University of Windsor, to study with Joyce Carol Oates, and then my Ph.D. from State University of New York–Binghamton, to work with John Gardner.

In school, I started writing stories that I think shared a certain kinship with my father's stories: they gave me a way to imagine myself in the world. And writing was a way to say the deepest sorts of truths that I had been taught it was not polite or reasonable for a young woman to speak out loud. Even in the safety of metaphor and imagery, I found I had to struggle to continually reach for my private reality. My first novel, *Arabian Jazz*, was a broadly humorous novel—which I hadn't intended or expected it to be. But the characters and the prose kept veering into comedy, which, as I look back on it now, seemed a "safer" sort of vehicle for this story. I'd never read a novel from an Arab American perspective before; I had no idea if Americans would be at all receptive to it. Humor emerged as one of the best and most immediate ways of connecting easily and intimately with my readers.

After graduate school, I taught creative writing, film studies, and contemporary literature at a number of different universities, including the University of Nebraska, the University of Michigan, the University of California–Los Angeles, and the University of Oregon. All of these places had something new to teach me about being an American. I moved around for work, but I think I also liked to move. While there's a certain rootlessness and solitude to nomadism, I suppose that I am, as my father asserts, fundamentally a Bedouin. I am driven to exploration and conversation despite my best efforts to sit quietly in one place. I would just as happily host a dinner party as give a reading, and my chronically social nature frequently disrupts anything like a real work ethic.

Even in my work, I am restless—while I'm prone to write novels, I am also crazy about writing restaurant and film reviews, interviewing politicians and profiling county fairs, and fantasizing about writing a great Arab American screenplay. My second novel, *Crescent*, rose in part from my fascination with food and rituals around cooking, eating, and gathering. Sirine, the chef in the novel, lives the alternative fantasy I had for myself when I was a child—to become a chef and work in a small restaurant, feeding all my friends. Another way my father taught us about our culture was through preparing the dishes of our ancestry. Every time Dad made us *mansaff*, or stuffed grape leaves, it brought us a little closer to the child he had been, and brought us closer as a family. My new book, *The Language of Baklava*, a food memoir, grows directly out of these memories and associations, and it uses my parents' recipes throughout the work.

My new idea is to live beside the ocean with my husband and my nervous little Italian greyhound, and to work outside under an umbrella with a pitcher of lemonade and a plate of cookies. Once again, I will attempt to settle down and write for hours and hours at a time, the way I am told one must. But I suppose that I will end up, as usual, inviting friends or family over so I don't eat all the cookies myself. We will sit outside together, contemplating our origins and destinations, and begin telling each other stories again.

Fiction

In the following excerpt from *Crescent*, Sirine, the protagonist, listens to a story her uncle tells her—it is a long and winding tale to which he adds new sections in each telling. Each chapter of *Crescent* begins with the latest installment of this tale. What follows is a scene from the developing romance between Sirine and Hanif (nicknamed Han), an Iraqi American professor, who will help her understand her own identity. However, Sirine discovers that there is more than one obstacle standing in the path of her relationship with Han.—SMD

Sir Richard Burton wandered the Arab world like a speckled wraith. He dressed in native garb, spent hours gazing into Arab eyes. Arabic, in turn, went into his heart like a piercing seed, growing tendrils of beliefs and attitudes. But his tongue was flat as slate. He spoke so many languages that he had no native music left in him. He did, however, like so many Victorians, have an aptitude for owndership, an attachment to things material and personal, like colonies and slaves—he especially enjoyed owning slaves while living in someone else's house. He was an amateur slaver but he was a professional amateur, wearing the robes of so many different tribes, eating the food and entering the land of so many different countries.

Burton had written a book called *The Perfumed Garden*, and after she sold herself to Burton, Abdelrahman Salahadin's mother Auntie Camille found herself in just such a place. Burton's house in Syria, where he was residing at the time, was loud with birdsong, splashy with butterflies; ladders rose into bowers, grapes swayed, trellises swung and vines clung, and the sky arched like the roof of a mosque. And there was Sir Richard sitting in the middle of it, crouching on cushions, fat as a pasha, with his friends and all the local yokels coming and going, talking, eating, forming opinions, messing up the paperwork, et cetera. Not like this so-called America today where they just talk all day long on their phone, their computer, and no one ever lays eyes on each other and no one remembers how to cook a tomato or to bring flowers or to kiss the babies.

Anyway, Sir Richard said to Auntie Camille, yes, it's true I know the way to the source of the Nile, I helped find it, but it no longer matters. I no longer want anything to do with that silly river. You see, Sir Richard's former best friend had grabbed all the credit for himself about finding the source, so Sir Richard's heart was no longer in it.

What does Camille do? Does she lose heart? Not in the least. She sits on a rug of leaves on leaves and that sound is a word and the word, she says, is *aujuba*, wonder. She watches the way the nightingales and the hummingbirds spin around the garden like spirits and shadows. She makes a house of the outdoors, a cape of the night. You may have guessed that she wasn't much of a slave, but that was of little consequence to Burton, who, remember, was just an amateur, and enjoyed collecting people just for the sake of collecting. He adorned himself with Arabs, Chinese, and Indians, and he wrote and wrote and wrote, trying to fill the empty space inside him with a layer of ink.

He also happened to be married. It was a marriage conducted at arm's length. But of course, as Chekhov said: if you fear loneliness the marriage is not for you. His wife was an agreeable soul who routinely burnt whatever writing of her husband's was not to her liking.

Well, it could not have escaped the notice of Mrs. Sir Richard that a coal-eyed beauty with shimmering hair had taken up residence on one of their terraces, and when she pointed this out to Mr. Sir Richard, he said vaguely, hm, oh yes, so she is, so she is. And when the Mrs. pressed for more information, he said, oh, mm, she's one of the slaves, dear.

But here is the interesting part. In her slow and very nice and deliberate way, Aunt Camille began to take up space in Burton's imagination. Like a creature leaving a chrysalis, she began the metamorphosis from slave to muse. He found he liked to contemplate her curled up on the lawn while he ate his morning scone and he liked to watch her peeling loquats while he worked on his conjugation of Croatian intransitives.

He was a slaver, an explorer, and a translator, yet he could not quite translate Camille's while Nile of skin and blue Nile of hair into the right sorts of words. She made him ache in seven different places and she taught him the seven kinds of smiles; she filled his sleep with smoke and made his mouth taste of cherries. And one day, after thumbing through some old notebooks, random tales from ancient Persia, Phoenicia, Hindustan, Burton found himself writing the thunderstruck phrase: "And afterwards." He had begun his famous, criminal, suggestive, imperial

version of Victorian madness dissolved in the sky over the Middle East—
his translation of *The Thousand and One Nights.*

* * *

That evening after work, while mockingbirds are singing loudly in the
branches and the palms tumble over her head in the breeze, their fronds
like crossed swords, Sirine walks to the Victory Market.

"Bonjour, honored chef!" Khoorosh cries out as soon as she enters. The
shop is small and close, the air damp with a rich influx of spices, garlic,
saffron, and clove. Sirine often shops there, even when she doesn't need
anything—just to sample a new spice or to taste one of Khoorosh's im-
ported ingredients, dreaming of new dishes located somewhere between
Iraq, Iran, and America.

"Chef, these I put aside, just for you," Khoorosh says, as he hurries to
the back of the store. He returns with preserved lemons, Turkish honey,
pomegranate paste, and a container of tiny apricots, and brings them to
the counter. "Look at these beauties," he says suavely. "The foods of love."

"Beautiful. How much are they?" Sirine asks.

"What are you talking about? You're insulting me now."

"Khoorosh, you can't always give me everything."

"No, these are a gift."

"I want to pay for my gifts."

"Never mind. These are a gift from my hand to yours. If you say one
more single word about money I'm going to become very upset. I'm
developing a headache now."

More customers come in and greet Khoorosh in Farsi, the language
rippling fluidly between them. Sirine flees back into the shelves, the intimate smoke of spices mixing with the sound of the customers' laughter.

She enjoys the refined cadences of Farsi, enjoys this eavesdropping
without understanding; it is comforting and delightful and deeply familiar—the immigrants' special language of longing and nostalgia. Her childhood was spent in places like the Victory Market, holding her uncle's hand
as they wandered in search of the special flavors that weren't in any of the
big American grocery stores. It didn't matter if the shop was Persian,
Greek, or Italian, because all of them had the same great bins of beans and
lentils, glass cases of white cheeses and braided cheeses, murky jars of
olives, fresh breads and pastries flavoring the air. And the shop makes her
think of Han—somehow, everything seems redolent, brimming with sug-
gestions of Han. When she turns into an aisle full of bins of red and yellow
spices and resinous scents that swirl through the air, she is swept by a
craving so thorough, she understands finally that she isn't getting sick. It
seems that something potent was unlocked inside her during the night, as
they shared sleep without quite touching, his breath fanning her face. The

intimate proximity of Han's body comes back to her now, the scent of his skin echoed in the rich powder of spices. Desire saturates her, filling her cells, and her sense of reserve instantly gives way. The sweep of her own hand through the air, the switch of her legs, even the rush of breath through her mouth stirs her. She hurried with her few supplies to the cash register, her head lowered and her hands fumbling with money, and pays for as much as Khoorosh will allow.

Sirine walks out then, forgetting her purchases, and Khoorosh has to run outside with her bag. She laughs breathlessly and tucks the bag into her bicycle basket, knocks back the kickstand, and heads into the star-sprinkled night. She's in a postwork haze, her joints loose, muscles slack, but she peddles until she's sweaty and breathless. She doesn't even know if Han will be home, but then he is there, opening the door and nodding as if in answer to a question. He puts her bag on the counter and looks at her. He moves a few steps closer, then, instinctively, shyly, she takes a few steps back. "Wait," she says. She removes a pint of apricots, plump and as exquisite as roses, and offers him one. He takes a bite and puts his hand over hers as she takes a bite, the velvety peel and fruit sugar filling her whole mouth. The air between them is complicated, infused with the scents from the bags: toasted sesame, sweet orange blossom water, and fragrant rosewater.

They finish it and she drops the apricot pit in the sink; Han cups her hand again and licks a drop of juice from her fingertip.

Sirine holds her breath; the ground gets a little wavy. Han slips behind her and runs his hands over the tops of her shoulders. He tilts the top of his head to the back of her head, squeezes, and begins rubbing the muscles between her neck and shoulders. Her head falls forward, captured by the pleasure of it. He presses the heels of his palms along her inner back and squeezes her shoulder blades and rubs just inside them. She lets him work his way down to the small of her back, then back up to the V between her shoulders. He strokes the sides of her rib cage, digs into the tight saddle of flesh over her shoulders, rubs the back of her neck, then runs his knuckles down the length of her back. He interweaves new strokes and pressures. After several deepening, luxurious passes, her body is boneless and liquid.

She turns in to him and they twine their arms around each other. They slide and kiss and Sirine tosses off her shoes. She dances him backward into the bedroom, backing down onto his mattress. They pull at each other's clothes, trying to unwrap each other, kicking at pants and tossing shirts. He pauses and carefully removes the yellow plastic barrettes in her hair. They roll over each other, stroke each other's arms and legs; he laces his fingers into hers. She opens her mouth and tastes his skin and tongue. He is amber and caramel and earth-colored. His skin excites her; she inhales deeply, as if she could take in his essence; he tastes of almond, of sweetness. She hesitates a moment, then says, "Do you have, you know—"

"What?"

"You know. Protection?"

His face goes blank and he says, "Protection against what?"

Then he smiles, rolls over to his discarded pants, and pulls a condom out of the pocket. He waves the plastic wrapper by one corner and says, "We're safe!"

The last time Sirine has had sex with anyone was with a tanned beach boy named Danny, over three years ago: long enough for her to have more or less forgotten the feeling of it. But now, when Han rocks his body over hers, the lean weight of his thighs rubbing against hers, it is practically a new sensation, the physical pleasure opening and stirring through her muscles. Her back arches and her ribs seem to unlock. He moves with a deep, almost animal assurance, seemingly without any self-consciousness at all: his body wholly engaged and his eyes steady and focused. She opens her mouth and the only sound is a rushing breath, sweeping through, expanding and contracting the room. They move together, watching each other, hands joined.

At the end, Han's eyes dilate and darken and his mouth opens as if in surprise but he makes no sound; the length of his body holds and contracts, softens and slowly collapses over hers. She presses in against him and then feels that she is falling through her body; her pulse is fast inside her chest. She finally shuts her eyes and feels the last riffling sensations beneath her skin, and then, briefly, has a sense much like leaving her body: rising just beyond their small balcony, seeing rows of balconies, pale streets, plaster houses the color of skin, neat red tile roofs. The violet night streaks across their faces. There are glistening palms, pool-dark salamanders between the houses, patient iguanas. She senses the insect world turning, horned beetles and wax-winged figures taking to the air. She opens her eyes into the damp, fever dream of their embrace.

Han's arms smell like bread and sleep; when he gathers her back, it is like being drawn into a world beneath the water, an undersea cave. She closes her eyes and floats. And eventually, still in his arms, she sleeps.

* * *

At points, her sleep feels heavy as the ocean, other times she rises near the surface and seems to hear odd sounds: small cries, untuned music. Or she glimpses cloudy faces, unknown apparitions. She feels vaguely that she is being watched.

Sirine wakes after just a couple of hours, in the early part of the dawn, and the apartment is filled with a silver fog. A country filled with milky canals. She walks to the door and looks back at Han and his face is smooth with sleep. His skin has taken on a bronze patina.

She walks around his small bedroom, naked and bleary-eyed, feeling like she's awakened into someone else's dream. There are objects scattered around: a few books inscribed with gold Arabic calligraphy, a glass bottle filled with colored sands, a string of beads, a folded-up square of silk, a brass letter opener, and beside this, a photograph in a silver frame: a younger Han beside a boy and young woman, each of them with the same nut-brown skin, chestnut-colored eyes. They look happy and complete and Sirine feels a vague jealousy over their apparent ownership of each other. She tries to remember if Han said he had a sister. She replaces the picture carefully beside the letter opener.

Drowsy, she is about to return to the warm cave of his arms and chest, but she pauses for a moment, listening. Did she just hear something? She stands in the doorway that faces out to the balcony and sees how the cardamom-scented fog is everywhere in the streets, as if it rose from the breath of dreamers inside the street of houses.

She turns to go back to bed but then a glint of something catches her eye. And she turns and it cannot be, but the darkness and the fog create the illusion of a gargoyle face peering into the window, as if someone were crouching in a corner of the balcony, watching.

She catches her breath. But she knows this must be a mirage, part of a dream. She closes her eyes and moves backward, slowly and carefully, until her leg touches the edge of the bed; she lowers herself in and lies there for a while, waiting for her mind to settle, telling herself, it's nothing, there's no one out there. She pulls the covers up tight around her neck, crawls in close to Han, and, after much turning and resettling, gradually falls back to sleep.

Language

The Coming Out of the Chameleon

Samia Serageldin

Introduction

Samia Serageldin was born and raised in Egypt; she left at the age of twenty to pursue a graduate degree at London's School of Oriental and African Studies. She grew up in a politically prominent family that was subjected under the revolutionary Nasser regime to confiscation of property, imprisonment, and surveillance. After earning her M.S. in Politics from the University of London, she returned to Egypt in 1977, where she witnessed the ephemeral optimism generated by Anwar Sadat's dramatic about-face in political and economic policy. In 1980, she left definitively for the United States.

Her first novel, *The Cairo House*, draws heavily on these autobiographical experiences. Published in 2000, it follows the story of Gihan, a young woman who returns to Egypt in the mid-nineties after a long absence, and her attempts to reconnect with her past and with the young son she left behind. It captures the political developments in Egypt over the past three decades, including the rise of Islamism and Sadat's assassination.

In addition to writing fiction, Serageldin is also the author of several publications on women and Islam in Egypt and Arab American writing. She has contributed essays and served as consulting editor on a book on globalization and international terrorism, *In the Name of Osama Bin Laden* (2002).

She lives in North Carolina where she teaches at Duke University and writes a newspaper column. She has completed a collection of short stories and is in the process of writing her second novel.

The French have a saying: "Happy people have no story." I wouldn't go that far. But it may be a blessing in disguise, for a writer, to have "lived in interesting times," as the Chinese curse goes. That I have done. I grew up in Egypt under a revolutionary regime at a time of great political and social upheaval; none were more affected than politically prominent, land owning families like my own.

But my memories of early childhood are those of a happily hybrid culture: Egyptian cuisine and French governesses; English schools and Nubian doorkeepers; celebrating the Muslim Feast of the Sacrifice and licking Italian ices on the beach in a swimsuit. Then one day, in the early sixties, this world came to an end. The Nasser regime's sequestration decrees designated certain families as "enemies of the people"; the men were whisked away to a camp for political prisoners; everything we owned was confiscated.

It was around that time that I became a compulsive reader: Enid Blyton's Famous Five series; the Comtesse de Ségur's stories; selections from Librairie Hachette's rose imprint, color-coded for age-appropriateness. Later, as I grew older, these would be supplanted by Walter Scott and William Makepeace Thackeray; George Sand from Hachette's green imprint; Stendhal and Honoré de Balzac from the black. I was the kind of child and adolescent who couldn't go anywhere without a book in hand, the kind who, temporarily bereft of reading material, would resort to reading the ingredients on sauce bottles and the labels on shampoo. Reality intruded feebly into my alternative universe of books. I remember raising my head from the mist-shrouded moors of *Wuthering Heights* and blinking in disoriented resentment at the blinding glare from the Mediterranean sun glancing off the water at the beach in Alexandria.

I also read in Arabic, but never as much, in spite of my father's best efforts to hook me on Jurji Zaidan's Mamluk epics, Naguib Mahfouz's bleak realism, Yussef El-Sibaei's romantic novels, or even Ihsan Abdel Kuddous's risqué short stories.

Every writer's relationship with books must surely start as a passive one, absorbing and internalizing, until the day you begin to create. I began writing sporadically as a teenager, entirely imaginary, escapist short stories, but also a few, surprisingly real, stark poems. But as I grew into a woman, I seemed to lose my voice.

At twenty I left for London to study at the university, and I have lived abroad in one place or another, more or less ever since. The years passed and I made a very different life for myself; my sons grew up playing ice hockey in Michigan and soccer in North Carolina. There was no room in this brave new world for my memories of jasmine and dust. I locked away my photo albums of Egypt in the attic and blended into my new environment like a perfect chameleon. Friends who knew me for years barely knew where I was born. There was no hypocrisy involved; only the need to compartmentalize in order to survive. When glimpses of my former life transpired like a palimpsest, I dreaded the slightly skeptical question that inevitably ensued: "So what are you doing here in Houghton (or Newton or Chapel Hill)?"

But I returned to Egypt constantly, in my mind, weaving my memories into stories that I stored away in that virtual filing cabinet all writers carry around in their heads. Later I went back, in the flesh, every few years. Every time, I was struck by the relentless pace of change sweeping the country; soon the last traces of the world I had known would be gone with the wind. My sons would grow up impoverished by ignorance of their heritage. And that was the impetus for putting the stories in my head on paper. But once I started writing, what was meant to be an exercise of recollection in tranquillity turned into a painful, highly personal struggle to reconcile my present with my past. I was recovering my lost voice.

Yet, when I finally did sit down at the keyboard to write *The Cairo House*, I did not produce a memoir. Editors pointed out the advantages: the powerful appeal of first-person testimony; the fact that memoirs are more marketable today than novels; that much of my material was autobiographical anyway; and other unassailable arguments along those lines. But I stuck to my guns. I knew that, in my case, a memoir would be less free, and in a very real sense less true, than a novel could be. In a memoir I could not avoid feeling under enormous personal pressure to circumvent anything that could be construed as offensive, libelous or scandalous, especially given the politically or personally sensitive nature of certain passages in the book. Moreover a memoir might well have been less interesting: only in a novel would one have the license to conveniently conflate two aunts into "Tante Zohra," for instance; or to explore "the path not taken," at a crucial juncture in the story. Finally, I confess that overcoming my natural reticence would have been altogether too daunting without the fig leaf of fiction.

I have been asked why, having grown up trilingual, I choose to write in English rather than, say, Arabic. The easy answer is that, having spent my entire adult life studying or living in Anglophone countries, English is now my dominant language. But I know the explanation is more complex and multilayered. By choosing to write in English, immigrant writers position themselves firmly on the side of their new reality in relation to their own identity and to the readership they address. Language, moreover, is an entire codification of culture and cultural inhibitions; what a writer may express freely in one language she may feel far too inhibited to find words for in another. Add to that the particularity of Arabic: all native speakers of Arabic are diglossic. Rendering dialogue spoken in colloquial idiom into literary Arabic becomes a matter of some difficulty and considerable artifice. Even when the author opts for transliterating the colloquial verbatim, the results are unsatisfactory. As a result, it can seem no more unnatural to render colloquial Egyptian, for example, in English than in literary Arabic.

But if most writers must come down on one side or the other when it comes to the choice of the language of expression, the hyphenated American maintains her bifocal vision: the insider/outsider perspective, with its privileges as well as its pitfalls. This dual vision comes at a cost; she is never completely at home in either culture, however perfectly integrated and comfortable she may appear in both.

When my first novel, *The Cairo House*, was published in November 2000, it came as a complete surprise to most people who knew me, since I had largely kept my writing to myself. The central metaphor of the book is that of the chameleon, the person who has more than one skin and is an expert at blending into more than one culture. In a very real sense, the publication of the book was a coming out of sorts for me: as an Egyptian, and as a woman with a personal history irreconcilable with her present life. The experience was overwhelmingly positive; I was particularly moved by the resonance of my writing with strangers who had never even been to the Middle East. In retrospect, it was a preparation for my second coming out, less than a year later, in very different and difficult circumstances.

I had always worn my Muslim identity lightly, taking it for granted but keeping it a purely private matter. After September 11, that was no longer possible. Today, Americans of Arab or Muslim heritage find themselves mediating multiple identities and considering various responses, ranging from disassociation to affirmation to reinterpretation. Muslim Americans of all stripes and varying degrees of commitment to their religious heritage are obliged, for better or worse, to bear the burden of shaping the collective image of what is erroneously perceived as a single community but is in fact a homogenizing label applied to people of highly diverse sensibilities and backgrounds.

Like many others, I took up my pen and took to the podium, writing and speaking against the demonization of Arabs and Muslims and the erosion of civil liberties. If my experience growing up in a police state taught me anything, it was to recognize incremental incursions on civil rights for what they are: a mortal danger to the very freedoms for which people like me had come to America.

For the very private person I have always been, it comes as a bitter realization that, in the post–September 11 world, there is no place for the chameleon to hide. Even the private world of the writer is inexorably politicized, with a new awareness that the nature of representations of Arabs in the media, in literature, and in the entertainment industry, are likely to have far-reaching consequences.

This comes at a critical time. Until very recently the absence of Arabs and Muslims as subjects in mainstream American fiction was compounded by a corresponding dearth of full-length fiction by writers of Middle Eastern heritage. But a critical mass is beginning to form with the flowering of a handful of novels and memoirs by immigrant and first-generation authors. The importance of fiction and narrative nonfiction lies in the unique, privileged space for empathy and identification on the part of the American reader.

These writers of Arab heritage, when asked, are likely to say that they do not give any thought to the literature of representation, but in the wake of September 11, they may feel more subject to inhibiting considerations. In particular, themes of sexuality and gender relations rarely escape the politics of representation, given that gender and sexual stereotypes contribute so significantly to the construct of Arab "exceptionalism." On the one hand, notions of the "appropriate" cultural posture expected of women of that heritage may inhibit some writers from realistic depictions of sexuality; on the other hand, the expectations of many publishers favor the portrayal of oppressive, patriarchal family dynamics in the writing of Arab or Muslim women. Yet it is interesting to note that writers resist this agenda: father/daughter relations in the writings of Arab women go against the grain of preconceptions, with fathers overwhelmingly portrayed in positive, supportive roles.

Another potential minefield is religion. The risk of reinforcing negative stereotypes and prejudices about Islam may weigh on the words of Muslim writers in particular. If I expected *The Cairo House* to evoke controversy in Egypt, and among Egyptian reviewers in the States, for its political views on past and current regimes, I was blindsided by the reservations expressed by some Egyptian readers about descriptions of Islamic practices such as the Feast of the Sacrifice. There were even some objections to the citing of verses from the Quran. There was some concern that these passages—although entirely inoffensive in my intention—would reflect negatively on Muslim culture in the eyes of "foreigners" who did not understand the religion.

This, it is worth noting, was nearly a year before September 11. Today, there may be more consciousness of the responsibility of representation among writers, and greater vulnerability to criticism, which would be an unfortunate and self-defeating attitude. Only literature unfettered by self-censorship, written "from the heart," warts and all, can transcend the limitations of "exceptionalism" and allow the mainstream reader to penetrate the cultural opaqueness of the "other."

It also remains to be seen, post September 11, the role that the politics of the literary marketplace will play, and whether Arab American writing will succeed in imposing itself in the long term. There may be a certain ephemeral fascination with the Middle East, driven by current events, a curiosity not devoid of stubborn misconceptions and set agendas. The challenge is to persuade the industry that fiction by Arab American authors can appeal to a mainstream readership as widely as fiction by other ethnic groups such as Latinos and Asians. Curiously, women's voices seem to dominate among writers of Arab heritage just as they do in other emerging ethnic genres.

As future works by Arab American writers follow a natural progression, they are likely to address themes of broader appeal. First novels tend naturally to be explicitly or implicitly memoirs in disguise, and are often an exploration of ethnic heritage. Second or third novels evolve away from heritage and Middle East settings, and turn to American locations and experiences. I have found that observation to hold true for my own writing. *The Cairo House* was largely autobiographical and largely set in Egypt. My forthcoming novel, and several short stories, reflect American actuality more than remembered worlds.

But even more basic, post–September 11, is the issue of relevance: if American writers in general experienced difficulty in rediscovering relevance in the themes of their writing, how much more of a struggle it is for those of Arab heritage to reengage, and to justify, the eternal, universal themes of the human condition: love and lust, family and fortune, fitting in and standing out. But only by continuing to write uncontrived, unmediated, uncensored narratives can they hope to offer a first-person, authentic perspective to counterbalance the fun house of mirrors that is the literary imaginary of the Arab and Muslim "other" in America today.

Fiction

The following is an excerpt (Chapter 1) of *El Greco*, a novel-in-progress.

Robert Bauer unfolds the scrap of paper in his hand, looks at it, folds it up again. He stares out the window in front of his desk, an Empire-style bureau plat that is meant to sit, imposingly, idle, its polished surface bare but for a leather blotter and an antique inkwell. As it is, it is cluttered with two telephones, a fax machine, framed photographs of Bauer's wife and son, a tray with a pitcher of water and two bottles of prescription pills. The answering machine hooked up to one telephone is programmed to kick in after one ring, the one hooked up to the other phone kicks in after three rings. Both numbers are unlisted.

Bauer unfolds the scrap of paper and studies it again, rubbing his beard. He pours himself a glass of water and swallows two pills. They upset his stomach but he can't function without them today. Nothing about his body seems to function lately: the revolt of the flesh after years of neglect, erupting in ulcers and acid, sores and night sweats. Could be partly psychosomatic, he is told. Depression. He cannot work up an appetite for anything, eating or sleeping, making love or making money.

He isn't supposed to take these pills on an empty stomach. He should tell the housekeeper to fix him a sandwich. He flips on the switch to the intercom in the kitchen and hears a muffled drone on the ground floor. Celeste is vacuuming. He flips off the switch and waits for her to finish. He looks at the number on the scrap of paper again. He has had it for two days now, exactly three days since Caroline Norton's party.

Caroline's parties were a triumph of deliberate eclecticism, Robert Bauer was thinking as he scanned the large rooms: a blend of old Boston, new money, and Cambridge academics, with a dash of international spice. His eyes slid back to the woman in the bare-shouldered black dress. Italian? Argentinean?

The man at his elbow interrupted his speculation. "This whole stock market crash—it's artificial in a way, computer driven. But the company itself is sound, that stock will rebound, I'm betting on it. It's an opportunity for someone who can afford to ride out the downturn."

Bauer had heard that enough times since Black Monday, October 19, almost two weeks ago. He shrugged.

"You know I retired last summer." He made it sound like a choice.

"I envy you, to be in a position to retire in your forties."

Through the French doors leading to the winter garden Bauer heard the woman in the black dress laugh. Caroline's latest young artist-in-residence, an Italian, said something to her and she turned so that her back was to Bauer. Her dark hair was loosely piled at the back of her head, a few strands trailing down her nape. There was something about the configuration of her neck that made Bauer want to feel his palm against it. He couldn't remember when a woman he had not even met had such an effect on him.

A blue-veined, ring-encrusted hand on his sleeve diverted his attention to Caroline. "Your Susan is a one-woman committee," she trilled. "Such energy! I don't know what we'd do without her. I simply must tell her about this Young Artists benefit." Caroline flitted off. He tried to stifle a yawn in his beard. He hoped his doctor knew what he was doing, prescribing these antidepressants.

The woman in black tipped her head back and looked around, presumably for her hostess. Her wide eyes met Bauer's for an instant and looked away. A tall dark man brought her coat. The couple headed toward the hall.

Bauer turned back to the drawing room that now seemed empty. He combed his fingers through his longish, sandy hair and straightened his heavy-set shoulders. Show's over, he thought, lights out, time to go home.

Suddenly he put down his drink, spilling it slightly on the marquetry top of the console table. "Excuse me," he interrupted the man who had been trying to interest him in French telecommunications technology, and headed for the hall.

The woman and her escort were gone. Caroline was still there with some other guests who were taking their leave. She was basking in their compliments, standing under a stunning portrait of herself painted some forty years ago. Whenever Caroline stood in front of that particular wall in the hall she almost unconsciously adopted the pose in the portrait, three quarter face, an elegant hand touching the emerald pendant at her throat.

"Robert, you're not leaving already? Where's Susan?"

"No, but I wanted to have a word with you about that Young Artists benefit you were looking for sponsors for. Shall we go into the library?"

"Egyptian? Really?" Robert Bauer raised his eyebrows. "She doesn't look Egyptian." He leaned against the mother-of-pearl inlaid game table in front of the bookcase.

Caroline eyed him nervously: "Isn't that the loveliest table? But very fragile, Syrian work, we bought it in Beirut when Henry was ambassador there. Very fragile, I really wouldn't—"

Robert shifted his weight. "What did you say her name was?"

"Nadine. Nadine Zirquany. Apparently she's Zirquany Pasha's daughter. He was a sort of *eminence grise* in the politics of the country, but he's dead now, I think. Or did she say she was his daughter-in-law? Most Middle Eastern women use their maiden names, but sometimes they use their married names, especially when they're abroad. It can be very confusing and—"

"Is she married?"

"Well it's my impression that she is, although that's not her husband, I mean the man with her tonight, he's her brother, or perhaps her brother-in-law, I'm not sure which. His last name is different but I didn't quite catch it. Of course he could be her brother-in-law, if Zirquany is her maiden name, or her brother if it's her married name, now have I got that right? Anyway you see what I mean."

"How do you know her, Caroline?"

"Well I don't, really, I hadn't met her before tonight. She called this morning to ask me if she could have a look at some of dear Henry's private correspondence, apparently she's working on a dissertation, or a book, or an article for a magazine, or something like that. Well, I was busy preparing for the party, but when she said her name, Nadine Zirquany, it rang a bell, and she seemed charming over the telephone, so I invited her. You know I always like to keep up my ties with that part of the world.

Cairo was my favorite of Henry's postings, after Beirut, of course, before this dreadful civil war broke out. Did I ever tell you about—"

"How long has she been in Boston?"

"Not long at all, I don't think, because she doesn't seem to know anybody here, I mentioned some friends in the expatriate community and she didn't know them."

Robert saw the butler in the doorway, trying to catch Caroline's eye.

"Tell me, Caroline, when will she be coming back to have a look at Ambassador Norton's letters?"

"Oh, Henry's letters. Well, she won't be, as a matter of fact, because I donated them all to the Fletcher School at Tufts just last month. I would have been glad to let her see them, but it's out of my hands now. But I'm sure she'll be in touch, at least a thank-you note for the party, she seems to have charming manners, and such a very attractive girl, don't you think? Yes, really quite charming. Shall I let you know if I hear from her again?"

The last few remarks were uttered in the same giddy, lilting trill that Caroline had adopted as a debutante well over fifty years ago, but the pace had slowed noticeably, a sign that Caroline was thinking. Robert didn't particularly want to give her the opportunity to ponder his sudden interest in this woman. Caroline was no fool.

"Don't bother, it doesn't matter in the least. Now about the benefit . . . "

Robert folds the scrap of paper in his hand and looks out of the window. The view outside is very different from the one that this same desk faced only a few months ago, before he sold his business. Robert looks out at the garden in the back of the house; the dead leaves drifting into the drained pool, the umbrellas folded over the tables on the patio, the shriveled geranium heads in the stone planters.

He should get a yard service, or a proper gardener, he thinks, instead of Professor Ilya. Russian ornithology professors do not make good gardeners. It is supposed to be a temporary arrangement, but there are not many jobs available for an elderly Soviet refugee who doesn't speak much English.

One ring. The man pushing the French Minitel telecommunications deal. Sounds interesting, but it would take too much energy. Robert does not pick up.

Three rings. Susan, suggesting he join her and some benefit committee for lunch. Sounds concerned, with an underlying note of irritation. He doesn't pick up.

One ring. His accountant. Sounds worried. Needs to speak to him quite urgently about an audit on back taxes. He doesn't pick up.

Three rings. Dr. Berenson. Reminding him this is the second appointment he's missed this week. Sounds concerned. Missing appointments is a bad sign. Robert doesn't pick up.

He puts the scrap of paper in his pocket. Is this what retirement is like? He doesn't know what he expected. Not having to take any calls. Not having to wear a watch. Time. Switching off the treadmill under his feet for the first time in his life. He stares out the window. A squirrel scrabbles up the tree in front of him.

Robert takes the small scrap of paper out of his pocket and unfolds it slowly. He picks up the phone and dials the number he has copied on the paper. Two rings.

"Hello?"

Robert is taken aback. Her voice is high and light. He expected it to be low-pitched and throaty, perhaps with a slight accent. This voice does nothing for him.

"Hello? Hello?"

He hangs up. He thrusts the scrap of paper into his pocket.

He picks up the phone and punches in Drew's number. Perhaps he can talk him into coming home from college for the weekend. He hasn't been back since fall semester started. There is no answer.

One ring. The stockbroker he was supposed to have lunch with today. Sounds like he is trying to hide his annoyance at being stood up. Robert doesn't pick up.

He takes the scrap of paper out of his pocket and dials the number again. This time her voice is more wary. "Hello?"

"Hi. This is Robert Bauer. We met at Caroline Norton's party last week?"

"Oh—yes. Excuse me, I didn't quite catch . . . ?"

"Robert Bauer. Caroline told me a little about your research, and that you're new to Boston. I may be able to help you meet some people."

"Oh, that's very kind of you." She sounds doubtful, Robert thinks with a grin, because she is trying to remember meeting him.

"Why don't you and your husband come over for coffee tomorrow morning? You can tell me a little about what you're working on. And Susan—my wife—would like to meet you."

"My husband's out of town right now."

"I'll expect you around ten o'clock? Let me give you the address."

"Tomorrow? Perhaps we could put it off till my husband gets back?"

"I'm afraid tomorrow might be the only time I have available for a while."

"All right, tomorrow then."

Robert hangs up. It was easier than he thought. She hadn't even asked him how he got her number.

For My Mother Who Gave Me the Words, and My Father Who Gave Me the Sound

Marian Haddad

Introduction

Born in 1962 in El Paso, Texas, Marian Haddad is a freelance writer and teacher based in San Antonio, Texas. She earned her M.F.A. in Poetry and Creative Non-fiction from San Diego State University, and she teaches English and Creative Writing at Northwest Vista College and Our Lady of the Lake University, both in San Antonio. She also offers creative writing workshops in the area. Fluent in Arabic, English, and Spanish, she has been a Visiting Writer at various schools and institutions.

The daughter of Syrian American immigrants, Haddad learned the love of language—both written and spoken—at an early age. She first started writing when she was six, when her Arabic-speaking mother asked her to translate from Arabic into English the letters she wanted to write to Haddad's brother, who was stationed in Vietnam.

Haddad's essays and poetry have appeared in *The Rio Grande Review*, *The Texas Observer*, *Writers without Borders*, *100 Texas Poets* (edited by Naomi Shihab Nye), and *Stories from Where We Live: The California Coast* (edited by Sara St. Antoine). Her first poetry collection, *Somewhere between Mexico and a River Called Home* was published in 2003.

Among her literary influences, Haddad counts William Carlos Williams, W. S. Merwin, Sharon Olds, Naomi Shihab Nye, Yusef Komunyakaa, Glover Davis, Heather McHugh, Louise Gluck, Walt Whitman, Emily Dickinson, and Henry David Thoreau.

I can't recall which language I spoke first: the English of my native-born country, America, or the Arabic of my ancestors, parents, and Syrian-born brothers and sisters. I grew up hearing both languages simultaneously, and both languages made their way into me and into our central El Paso, Texas, home.

I remember being six years old, my mother calling me in Arabic to the living room coffee table. I'd come, sometimes reluctantly, sometimes gladly, to our chocolate brown wooden coffee table, sit on the floor, Indian-style, me and my paper and my pen, there in the early evening light, my mother sitting on the golden green stitched sofa near me, my head near her knees. This was the way we did it. This was the way she spoke to my brother Albert (Abdallah) in Vietnam. All I knew was that he'd gone away to this strange place; I didn't really know when he'd come back, I just assumed he would.

Mother was unable to write in English, and she had not yet taught herself to write in Arabic. So I was her arm, her language. She began dictating her nightly words, and I, barely six years old, began to write them down the best way I knew how. And it became apparent, even at six, that translation from one language to another would be difficult but doable. I knew I would falsify her words if I merely gave a rough translation, and that was not acceptable. Even as a child, something inside me knew that the spoken or written word in any language was holy, something holy about words. I knew they were truth, and therefore, I had to keep them there, in that sphere of truth and intention and time. And even though idioms in the Arabic language rarely find their equivalent in English, I made sure I got Mom's words across, the exact way she meant them to be received. I would translate verbatim, what she trusted me to write. "My Dear Abdallah, my oldest, my beautiful son. You are my heart. You are my eyes," and me, there, trying my hardest to say what it was she needed him to hear. She continued, "The walls of the house are weeping for you." It was then, during these moments, that Mother had become, and would prove to be, my daily giver of words. She gave them to me like candy, like different-colored pebbles, many shapes and sizes. She instilled them in me, met me there, in that place we called ours, in that place where two languages merged and where words somehow gave her hope.

We *had* to write the letters, even if she wasn't sure they would make their way to him. Even though she could not create the written characters, she was a writer too; she needed to go through the motion and reason for writing. She wrote to keep him alive, there in the bigger world, the one that reached past our safe turquoise house on North Virginia. And she passed that on to me, that need for the word, the wonderful way of figurative language, the sheer poetry of it, there in that living room, me sitting on the faded carpet, her on the sofa, the one Jiday Abdallah, her father, used to sit on when he came to America once to visit us all the way from Jawaikhat, his little Syrian village of orchards and apples. He was tall and lanky and had a five o'clock shadow, no matter the time of day. He'd play there, on that same table, Solitaire, slowly turning the cards, licking his forefinger, turning them again. But now, it became our spot, Mother and me. Our evening ritual, to visit my brother, there, in that dim place. She hardly slept. It made her somehow feel better, to keep him there in that house through words, through speaking his name in air, sending it out into our sphere, waiting for me to catch it, write it down, to inscribe him into our daily lives—words keep things in the present.

And it is in that present that my father spoke the sound. Barely educated in his home country, he gave up school to take care of his widowed mother, to help her in the fields. He had learned to write in Arabic through elementary school, had found the words there, in literature, in the Psalms, and then he had to leave them awhile. But there in that El Paso house, years later, he wrote poetry as a way of remembrance, as a way of honoring the living and the dead. I remember him at the kitchen table in our second home on Georgia Place. I was ten when we moved. He would sit under that kitchen lamp that hung above the brown and ivory Formica table, orange light making its way down onto him. He was golden there, his head bent over paper, him intent on creating; and he would read aloud, clearly, without restraint, in a metered tone, the words. Sometimes he'd speak them quietly, a near whisper, delicately searching out the sound. He'd revise, rerhythm, and read again. And so he, there in that kitchen, there in that light, had become my generous giver of sound, as he spoke it there in near constancy. I grew up hearing the cadenced, metered lines, his long *e*'s and his careful Arabic rhymes.

He repeated words, like water trickling behind our conversations and housework and homework. It was background music for me, even though I didn't know it then. I would be loading the dishwasher, making coffee for the uncles who were coming shortly to play cards, slicing oranges and apples for the fruit tray, wiping down the counters, preparing silver trays that held long, tall glasses of ice for the Coke and 7-Up. Or whether I was just walking down the hall. I heard him, often, nearly singing, his inflections well placed, his movement, well paced.

And then, when the big events came, he would orate in front of crowds, him standing proudly in front of the mike, there with his paper positioned crisply and erect in front of him. Wherever it was, Dad held the attention of the crowd, not speaking until all were quiet, making a way for the word, a certain kind of reverence. And it was there, at these functions, at a wedding, a baptism, the arrival of a relative from the old country, a party at our home, even a funeral, that I heard the quiet poem come into its fullness, there, with people attentive and listening, there, with those he'd made ready to receive.

My father would practice first at the house; he'd beckon us all to gather around the table: "Um Abdallah, Murrien, *kilkon itt-aou.*" And we would sit there and listen, gathering around what he'd written and the regular rhythms of his voice delivering.

And so this is my tradition, this is the way in which I was raised, to love words, to love their sound, their movement, their lyrical way. I was taught by my mother first to create the meaning, or to find it, find it through a simile, a metaphor, through personification, "Abdallah, the walls of the house are weeping for you." I will never forget that line. I thought it was miraculous that the walls of the house could weep. I thought it was pertinent that they should, since they housed my mother who cried silently at night, standing by her red roses that Albert somehow sent. So she taught me then, so many things, the translation of tongues, the sacredness of word choices, the miracles of words themselves, my first friend and finder of figurative language; and she instructed me, through our nightly letters to our far-away brother and son, to deliver them in the fullness of their meaning, to sew words together like blankets that covered us. And it was my father who taught me, then, to try to stitch them, tightly, seamlessly, fluidly, to hold them together somehow, to hold them together like snow, tightly packed like smaller particles that composed a greater part, small pieces sculpted together to form a larger field where every let-ter or sound counted, every phrasal tendency, every stress, the up and down of them, to love them and the sound they made, to send them into the air singing.

Poems

Monologue to My Father

As it is, Father, marriage scares me.
I know you wait to clutch my arm,
walk me down some long-awaited aisle,
give me to a man—a gift—some sacrifice.

You have braceleted my wrist with gold,
21 karat, spun in Syria, a gift you and Mother
purchased years back, afraid to not exist
'til then, gifting me one night with a wish

that I would find the man who would
complete me. I am still waiting, Father,

for that one who you said would come. Thirty-
seven and counting, Father. I have loved.

And still, I have not had the courage
to make a stay. I have no fortitude,
only fear that I will be encircled,
enslaved, some kind of trap.

How can I give my flesh, pledge
my spirit, my center of fertility,
to one man? Will he be with me till death?
And how long is that, Father? Who is to say

he'll stay? Who is to say I will?
I am a cavern and a cloud. Who can fill
or hold me? I am afraid, Father,
I may not marry. But if it be my state

to approach this union, then may you live
to guide me down that aisle, push the tulle
gently from my face, kiss the daughter's cheek
you give to a man you would entrust to bear me.

Durazno Street
El Paso, Texas

It's not like I know that much about you.
I never paid attention to the houses
on your street. Or the businesses
that lined your long South El Paso row.

But I know the name well. I used
to hear my father at the kitchen table
speak in a tongue I was still not familiar
with. He spoke quickly—and I knew

he was asking for directions. A great
thing to ask for. Direction. And I heard
words I would identify during each call.
Compadre. Hay esta listo. Para la bono.

He was always good with people. He had
to be to keep the house. Coming from Syria,

at 45, 8 children already born,
me on the way, a wife and mother to feed.

I remember the boxes of fruit and vegetables
he would buy at the restaurant supply, store
them in the back room, where it was colder
than the rest of our house. None of this

two heads of lettuce and a bag full of apples
at a time. There were crates of cantaloupe
with their rough and dusty skins, pears by
the bin, lettuce in its round fat body with

its blanket of crinkled leaves, and the avocados,
my favorite box. They sat there like stones,
a stone inside them. And I wouldn't even have
to mash them up. I would grab one in my hand,

the cold bumpy feel of it, the shape felt good
in my palm. And I would carry it to the kitchen,
cut it in half, and scoop it out with a spoon
and eat it that way. I did not need to slide

the steel fork down into it, add garlic and lime,
I ate it raw, the feel of it in my hungry mouth. The
taste of it on the tongue. And still, when I see
3 *Avocados for a dollar,* something in me leaps.

And I do the same thing. Eat it like the day
I heard my father say, *Durazno* over the kitchen
phone while I was at the sink, *Tularosa.* Streets
where the houses were, where he would pick

up his payments from his *compadres* for things
he would sell. He sat at the table with his *tarjetas,*
cards that held an accounting of what Jesus Ramirez
bought, and how much Jesus paid each time

my father would show up at his door. Three
weeks ago, in my rental car, I drove in that white
sun I love so much, down Montana, left on Piedras,
and there it was, Durazno, up on a big green sign,

a word from our kitchen table, a word I grew up
hearing, a familiar tone amidst the Spanish I
did not know then, a name I opened like the fruit
I picked from the back room of that house.

April 13, 2002
5:30 a.m.

For Naomi Shihab Nye

Granddaughter
of Sitti Khadra,
I did not know you
until I picked
your book off a shelf
twelve years ago.

It's there I first read
about your yellow glove,
a red suitcase, your Uncle
Mohammad and the broom-
maker in Palestine,
the way you made it seem
he was a master
of this one lost art,

how he woke up
and began to weave
the seam around the straw
stitched it into place,
taking such care,
as if it were something
his own wife would wear.

The way I saw your name
and it rang clear,
something in it meant
you were quite like me.

A name—how we relate
to people from our lands,
though I still

have mine, but you
do not
have yours.
Syria is still
on the map,
and last month
it resonated loud
and clear, your Palestine
has been
erased
from the map
on my friend's
wall.

For some reason, it was then,
I began to study
where every country lay,
and something in me sought
the places of my race,

and I began to see
the space between
Syria and Lebanon,
and how it was O.K.—
the separate countries
that they made,
allowed the other
to exist;

I looked for Jordan,
Yemen, The United
Arab Emirates.
Morocco and *El Jazayer*,
Berber countries first,
how they embraced
the same language
our grandfathers
spoke, but they, still
able to keep
their own identities.

I saw Israel
and thought,

Our neighbors, a part of us,
our space. A cup of sugar please.

And for a moment I forgot
a strange happening. I began to look
and look for one
country
I once had to name
on an old map.

My eye began to scan
the crevices in-between,
and a panic began
to stir somehow
inside the brain.

Unable to find
this one lost patch
of land, what color
was it then?

And the next second
it came to me. The way
it's been erased.

Oh, yes. I cannot even place
my finger atop
it's geographical brow,
the hump it might have made
under a braille hand
on the raised surface
of a sky blue globe.

It then made strange sense
to me, why I couldn't find it
between it's cluster
of neighboring spots.

I was appalled to think
someone had buried it
while I wasn't looking
straight, and that I didn't go
to this one funeral

they must have had
somewhere
to mourn their dead.

We hear so often
on the news, a story
somehow far away,
and we
forget to place
this one reality
in our own
dark book,

until something wakes us
into shock, and me pointing
my fleshy finger
on a land I once knew
existed there, cancelled
out. What about Sandy,
and Paul, my brother's friend,
his father's father came
from there, her grandfather left
it for L.A., and now,
there is no finding it
again. The place from which
they stemmed
has blown up, city
of smoke, and the houses
they once villaged in,

playing the nigh and the durbuk,
villages where weddings took,
and church bells rang,
or the call to prayer
in a mosque,

the children
playing with sticks
in thin alleys
between houses,
the women
baking the *sej*
and picking mint

out of their own
small yards.

Let It Be Each Day

Let it be each day I write

words, take them into me
like bread, bread of my being,
rising. Let it be each day

I put down my pen on sheets,
cut from wood, the bed that brings
each word a body, caterpillars bursting
in air. Let it be words that crown

me, encircle the temple
where they are born, hover
around the body
of their making. Let it be

words rising out
of my mouth, eyes, ears,
let me be covered
in the flurry of them. Let me

lie naked there, as in new
mown grass. Let me slide
in their silkweed, in their song,
in the hour of their waking.

Index

About the Contributors

ELMAZ ABINADER teaches writing at Mills College in Oakland California. Her first book, a memoir, *The Children of the Roojme: A Family's Journey from Lebanon*, was published in 1991. She has performed her plays in many venues across the country. Her poetry collection, *In the Country of My Dreams*, won the Josephine Miles PEN Oakland Award for multicultural poetry.

DIANA ABU-JABER won the Oregon Book Award for her first novel, *Arabian Jazz*, which was published in 1993. Her second novel, *Crescent*, was published in 2003. Her memoir, *The Language of Baklava*, will be published in 2004.

ETEL ADNAN's poetry and fiction has been widely published. Her novel, *Sitt Marie Rose*, has been translated into many languages. She divides her time between California and Paris, France, where she continues to pursue her writing and art.

BARBARA NIMRI AZIZ worked as an anthropologist for many years before turning to journalism, focusing her attention on the Arab lands and the Arab/Muslim community in the United States. Her weekly radio program, *Radio Tahrir*, airs over Pacifica-WBAI 99.5 FM in New York City (www.wbai.org). She produced an audio series, *Six Arab American Poets*, in 1997, and is working on further productions. In 1992, Aziz cofounded the Radius of Arab American Writers, Inc. and is currently its executive director.

SUSAN MUADDI DARRAJ is a freelance writer, editor, and teacher. She lives and works in Baltimore, Maryland, and is the editor of *The Baltimore Review*, a literary journal. Her fiction, articles, and essays have appeared in *Full Circle, New York Stories, Calyx*, the *Christian Science Monitor*, the *Monthly Review*, and elsewhere. Her book, *The Inheritance of Exile: Stories from South Philly*, was a finalist in the 2003 AWP Book Award Series for Short Fiction.

MARIAN HADDAD teaches English and Creative Writing at Northwest Vista College and Our Lady of the Lake University, both in San Antonio, Texas. Her work has appeared in various journals, as well as anthologies, including Milkweed Edition's *Stories from Where We Live: The California Coast* (edited by Sara St. Antoine), *Is This Forever or What?: Poems and Paintings from Texas* (edited by Naomi Shihab Nye), and *Arab American and Diaspora Literature* (edited by Nathalie Handal). Her first collection of poetry, *Somewhere between Mexico and a River Called Home*, will be published in 2004.

SUHEIR HAMMAD is a poet and the author of *Born Palestinian, Born Black*, and *Drops of This Story*. Hammad's work has received numerous awards and has been published in many anthologies and publications. Hammad is an original writer and cast member of the Tony Award–winning *Russell Simmons Presents Def Poetry Jam on Broadway*.

NATHALIE HANDAL is the author of numerous plays, of the poetry book, *The NeverField*, and the poetry CD *Traveling Rooms*. She edited *The Poetry of Arab Women: A Contemporary Anthology*, an Academy of American Poets best seller and winner of the Josephine Miles PEN Oakland Award. She teaches at Columbia University in New York City.

DIMA HILAL's work has appeared in various literary journals and anthologies, including the *San Francisco Chronicle, Mizna*, and *The Poetry of Arab Women: A Contemporary Anthology*. She is currently writing a libretto in conjunction with the Oakland East Bay Symphony's *Words & Music Project*. Hilal lives in Dana Point, California, where she is completing her first collection of poetry.

MOHJA KAHF teaches at the University of Arkansas in Fayetteville. Her first collection of poetry, *E-mails from Scheherazad*, was published in 2003. Her critical writing has appeared in various academic journals, and her poetry has been published in such forums as *The Paterson Review* and *The Space between Our Footsteps*, edited by Naomi Shihab Nye. She won an Arkansas Arts Council Award for her poetry in 2002.

GHADA KARMI is a research fellow at the Institute of Arab and Islamic Studies, University of Exeter, England. Her memoir, *In Search of Fatima: A Palestinian Story*, was published in 2002. She is often featured in the British and Arab media and also contributes articles on Middle Eastern subjects to *The Guardian*, *Al Hayat*, *Al Ahram Weekly*, and *Middle East International*.

LISA SUHAIR MAJAJ writes poetry and creative nonfiction as well as literary and cultural criticism. She has also coedited three collections of literary essays. Her creative work has appeared in such forums as *Mizna*, *Al Jadid*, *The Poetry of Arab Women* (edited by Nathalie Handal), *The Space Between Our Footsteps* (edited by Naomi Shihab Nye), and the *South Atlantic Quarterly* (the award-winning issue *Palestine America*).

NAOMI SHIHAB NYE writes poetry and prose. She has written and/or edited over twenty books, including the poetry collections, *Fuel* and *Red Suitcase*, the young adult novel *Habibi* and the collection *The Space between Our Footsteps: Poems and Paintings from the Middle East*. She lives and writes in San Antonio, Texas.

SAMIA SERAGELDIN'S first novel, *The Cairo House*, was published in 2000. In addition to writing novels, she has published widely on Arab American issues, as well as on Islam and Egypt. She contributed to and served as a consulting editor of *In the Name of Osama Bin Laden*, a collection on globalization and terrorism, which was published in 2002. She teaches at Duke University in Durham, North Carolina.